*To Educate a Nation*

*Autobiography of
Andres P. and Jane V. Enriquez*

## Praise for *To Educate a Nation: Autobiography of Andres P. and Jane V. Enriquez*

When I heard about this book revealed by Mr. Jeremy Enriquez, I was elated. I have long desired such enlightenment to be brought to the people of Belize about this great contribution of her people. I grew up with my parents as the teacher's daughter. Now thanks to *To Educate a Nation: Autobiography of Andres P. and Jane V. Enriquez*, edited by Mr. Jeremy Enriquez, valuable memories have come back to me and I feel part and parcel of the history of education in Belize. This book is indeed our story.

I am the daughter of Joseph Pollard Palacio and Hilaria Mejia Palacio. My father was also a school teacher. He taught at villages in Toledo, such as Santa Teresa and Aguacate, and in the Corozal District in the village of Sarteneja. Along with my family, including my brother, Theodore Joseph Palacio, now deceased, who also became a teacher, I experienced traveling through the Temash River and then walking a few miles to the village of Santa Teresa. Being a child at that time perhaps I was shielded from some of the hardships that my parents may have endured. I recall, however, that when my mother fell ill with typhoid and died in Punta Gorda Town after the 1945 Hurricane, it took several days for my father to get the news and then to travel to town. He arrived days after she was buried.

I am able to draw parallels in my experiences with those I read about in this book. I recall being able to interact well with the school children. I learned how to speak whatever language was spoken by the inhabitants of the villages. Therefore, along with my father and brother, I can speak Kekchi, Mopan Maya, Spanish, and, of course, Garifuna and English. I helped my father teach the infants when I had completed Standard 6 and at times I have been asked to go to court in town to be an interpreter for the Maya.

There were also times when my father decided to take a break from teaching and stayed in his home village, Barranco, for months to engage in farming and fishing with his relatives. He would then go again into teaching, probably because he was asked to return, but would keep up his fishing and farming during school holidays.

I must not forget to mention that Mrs. Jane Enriquez was really a great midwife and healer. Were it not for the herbal remedies and the massages that Mrs. Enriquez gave me, I would have only two children instead of four. I remember hearing that Mr. Enriquez was a great teacher and parent, and a fun-filled person. He and his wife spoke Garifuna, English and Mopan Maya at home.

Olivia Avila nee Palacio<br>Punta Gorda, June 2017

In the 1910s Punta Gorda had a growing number of able-bodied Garifuna men with the qualifications that the church fathers were looking for—strong and hardy to undergo the physical strain of walking miles through bush trails, the discipline to stay for months without basic amenities, while being very bright with an additional aptitude for teaching. Andres Patricio Enriquez was such a candidate.

In the book, *To Educate a Nation: Autobiography of Andres P. and Jane V. Enriquez*, editor Jeremy Enriquez adroitly brings out the basic quality that held his grandfather together under such intense sociocultural conflicts. It was his underlying faith in God that each calamity was a test he would overcome, God willing. His unqualified success came from gradually gaining the confidence of his host community to the extent that they kept asking for him to return several times after he had been transferred.

The section written by his grandmother Jane Victoriana Enriquez nee Villafranco is three times longer than that of his grandfather. The extra space abounds to the benefit of the reader. It is rare that the experiences of a woman intimately involved in teaching in remote rural communities has been exposed. As the pivot of her family, Jane's sensitivity extends widely from being mother, a woman who engaged in several domestic chores daily, such as food gathering in the field, and its preparation. She was a friend to women, young and old, and many other roles she executed daily, many times subconsciously. She gradually deepened her skills in healing using Maya and Garifuna practices. She had a sixth sense, a premonition to be able to foresee events. With all of these qualities, Jane remained an uncompromising support to her husband.

My own Palacio-Arana family is related to Andres and his wife. I remember visiting their family home in Punta Gorda as a child. From 1949 to 1951 I was in San Antonio with my brother Theodore J. Palacio, who was the school principal. I experienced minimally some of the culture shock mentioned in the book. And, as a son and brother of Garifuna teachers, I am aware of the movement from village to village that teachers and their families were forced to undergo. Such transcultural episodes became transfixed in my own growth.

Jeremy was able to augment these diaries with wonderful photographs and rich research from archival material. This book highlights his grandparents as most exemplary and compassionate human beings. In their abode in Seiri (the Garifuna name for heaven) Andres and Jane are proud of him and continue to smile at him with love and deep approval.

Joseph O. Palacio
Barranco Village, July 2017

# Dedication

This book is dedicated to Kahlil, Inaru, and Kareem Enriquez, and all the other descendants of Andres and Jane Enriquez.

> *Walking, I am listening to a deeper way.*
> *Suddenly all my ancestors are behind me.*
> *Be still, they say. Watch and listen.*
> *You are the result of the love of thousands.*
> —Linda Hogan

If you look deeply into the palm of your hand, you will see your parents and all generations of your ancestors. All of them are alive in this moment. Each is present in your body. You are the continuation of each of these people. —Thich Nhat Hanh


# Other Garifuna Books published by *Producciones de la Hamaca:*

Marcella Lewis, 1994. *Walagante Marcella: Marcella Our Legacy.*

Joseph O. Palacio, Carlson John Tuttle, and Judith R. Lumb, 2011. *Garifuna Continuity in Land: Barranco Settlement and Land Use 1862 to 2000.*

Carlson John Tuttle, 2012. *Bibliographical Collection on the Garifuna People.*

Michael Resman, 2012. *Lílana Ageiraü: The Villagers.*

Carlson John Tuttle, 2015. *On This Day in Barangu: A Genealogical Calendar of Life Events.*

Harriett Arzu Scarbough, 2015. *I Sing Barranco.*

# To Educate a Nation

## Autobiography of
## Andres P. and Jane V. Enriquez

Jeremy A. Enriquez, Editor

Copyright © 2017 Jeremy A. Enriquez

Other than as permitted by law, no part of this publication may be reproduced, stored in a retrieval system or transmitted, in any form by any means, without the prior written consent of the publisher.

Published by *Producciones de la Hamaca*
Caye Caulker, BELIZE
 <producciones-hamaca.com>

ISBN: 978-976-8142-97-9 (print edition)
ISBN: 978-976-8142-98-6 (e-book edition)

Thanks to the following sources for photographs and maps:

Andrew Enriquez, pages: front cover, xiv, 8 (*bottom*), 9 (*middle*), 28, 30, 56, 57, 60, 98 (*both*), 160

Belize Archives Department, pages: 8 (*top*), 9 (*top*), 24 (*top*), 61 (*bottom*), 69, 91 (*bottom*), 96 (*all three*), 97 (*both*), 106, 131 (*both*)

Carlson Tuttle Collection from the Jesuit Archives in St. Louis, Missouri, pages: 5, 16, 17, 24 (*top*), 34, 35 (*both*), 41, 43, 61 (*top*), 78, 91 (*top*), 105 (*both*), 120 (*both*)

Jeremy Enriquez page 24 (*bottom*), 173

Judy Lumb, pages: 19, 71

Royal Commonwealth Society, Cambridge Library, page: 65

Royal Geographical Society, page: 9 (*bottom*)

***Producciones de la Hamaca*** **is dedicated to:**

—Celebration and documentation of Earth and all her inhabitants,

—Restoration and conservation of Earth's natural resources,

—Creative expression of the sacredness of Earth and Spirit.

# Contents

Foreword .................................................................. ix
Preface .................................................................. xiii
Acknowledgements .................................................. xvii

**Introduction** ........................................................... 1
   Historical Background ............................................. 1
   Garinagu Arrival and Settlement in Southern Belize ....... 1
   Foundation of the Catholic Education in Belize ............ 6
   Role of Garifuna Teachers in Catholic Education in
      Belize ............................................................. 16
   Andres Patricio Enriquez 1886-1951 ......................... 18
   Other Outstanding Garifuna Teachers ....................... 22
   Impacts of Garifuna Teachers on the Development of the
      Catholic Church ............................................... 23
   Endnotes ........................................................... 25

***Au le, Andres Patricio Enriquez*** .............................. 27
   A Summary of the Teaching Service of Andres Enriquez ... 50
   Carib Teachers Proud Over Brother Teacher's M.B. E........ 52
   Supplement to the London Gazette .......................... 53
   MBE Says "Thanks" ............................................... 53
   Teacher M.B.E. in P.G. ........................................... 54
   Teacher M.B.E. Dies .............................................. 54

***Nuguya, Jane Victoriana Enriquez nee Villafranco*** ... 55
   San Antonio ....................................................... 60
   Christmas Vacation .............................................. 70
   Return to San Antonio ......................................... 72
   Traveling to and from Punta Gorda ........................ 78

| | |
|---|---|
| Garifuna Wood-cutters Visit San Antonio | 81 |
| Christmas Holidays 1913-14 | 83 |
| Alcalde Election in San Antonio | 84 |
| Travel by Rio Grande / House in Punta Gorda | 86 |
| Peacefully Settling a Village Argument | 86 |
| Priest Visits | 87 |
| Influenza at Rancho | 88 |
| El Cayo de San Ignacio | 90 |
| More Sad News in Punta Gorda | 95 |
| Progreso Village | 99 |
| Farewell to Progreso Village | 117 |
| Barranco | 119 |
| TOPCO | 122 |
| Crique Sarco | 132 |
| Return to San Antonio Village, Toledo District | 136 |
| My Call to Heaing | 140 |

## *Appendices*

| | |
|---|---|
| Appendix 1: Some Pupils of Andres P. Enriquez | 157 |
| Appendix 2: Family Charts | 161 |
| Appendix 3: History of the Early Settlement of San Antonio Village | 166 |
|     Geographic Description of San Antonio | 170 |
| Editor Jeremy A. Enriquez | 173 |

# *Foreword*

I think I was the Education Officer in Toledo when I first heard that the grandmother of Jerry A. Enriquez had kept a journal of her experience as a teacher's wife, an experience that spanned close to half a century and took the family to rural communities south, north and west of Belize. I had heard my parents speak of Teacher Peck as Jerry's grandfather, Andres Enriquez, was called in the Garifuna community, but never of his grandmother, Jane. I knew that she was the mother of Nurse Zenobia Palacio Nee Enriquez, whom my family credits with saving the life of my sister Judith Cayetano when, as a three year old, she had a life-threatening case of bronchitis. I had heard rumours that the good nurse, who was highly regarded in Barranco, had learned traditional medicine from her mother.

I later came to know two other sons of Andres and Jane Enriquez: Jerry's father, Solomon, a former primary school teacher who I understand was often called upon to serve as an interpreter of Maya at the magistrate's court in Punta Gorda and the Supreme Court in Belize City, and the youngest son, Constantine, who became a colleague when I joined the Ministry of Education as an Education Officer in 1976. As a teacher's son, and one who has done graduate work in linguistics, I marvelled at the high level of proficiency that all these Garifuna persons had in Mopan Maya and, as I later found out, several other languages as well.

Jerry, in a casual conversation, confirmed to me that his grandmother had indeed left a manuscript chronicling the experience of her husband and her family after her marriage to Andres Enriquez in 1912 and that he had it in his possession. While I did not have the good fortune of seeing the original manuscript, I was confident that it had to be something worth sharing with all of Belize and persons elsewhere and I promptly encouraged him to get it published.

At least fifteen years later, *To Educate a Nation: The Autobiography of Andres P. and Jane V. Enriquez* is being published. To me this is great news indeed. As editor, Jerry A. Enriquez has done an excellent job of preparing the material and introducing it with a section that sets the background that lays out the role of the Roman Catholic Church and the promising Garifuna young men they hand-picked to educate Belize. Younger Belizeans may not be aware of it, but older folks know that up to at least the start of the 1970s this country was educated primarily by Garifuna teachers. What is not so well known and appreciated are the day-to-day challenges confronted by the teachers and members of their families, and the high cost that they and their communities of origin had to pay for the privilege of delivering that service.

The second section is a moving summary of his life and teaching service by Andres Patricio Enriquez. This service of 48 years ended in illness and some heartbreak, but also the gratitude and appreciation of a government that awarded him with the MBE (Member of the Order of the British Empire) on behalf of King George VI, as well as the approbation of fellow teachers in 1950.

Finally, we come to the third and final section, the story as seen through the eyes of Jane Enriquez nee Villafranco, who married and joined her husband at the tender age of sixteen. Her journal covers all but the first eleven years of a remarkable teaching career and life in remote rural communities—bereft of basic amenities that we take for granted today—all in the service of the church and the country that did not always show their gratitude. This is the longest and to me the most intriguing section of the book, the true meat of the matter.

I can relate to every detail of this fascinating story because I, like the sons, daughters, wives and other relatives embedded in teacher families living away from home in the old days, have lived it. It is also my story and that of my father, my mother and my first three siblings. One of my earliest recollections is of Maya men from Santa Teresa, Toledo, being sent by the alcalde to pick us up in Barranco (or sometimes in Punta Gorda) and paddle to the mouth of the Moho River and then up stream, camping on the banks of the river before arriving at the landing and still having to trek another several miles to the village. I can still see the men catching iguanas to extract their eggs for our nourishment as we camped along the way and I cannot forget the texture and taste of *koretch*, a corn tortilla dried to last, kind of like the Garifuna *ereba* (cassava bread). I remember also the long walks when we had to undertake the journey in and out by road and how, just as in the case of Mrs. Enriquez, my own mother got much needed ease when she adopted the K'ekchi Maya way of carrying my then baby sister, Lorna, on her back in a cloth hammock hanging from her forehead.

I see some parallels between the life and work of Andres Enriquez and my father Eugene Cayetano. Like him, my father served in remote villages including San Antonio, Toledo, and in the closing years of his career was recognized for his outstanding service and awarded the MBE. But oh, how times had changed! While we had to walk to get to Santa Teresa and a much shorter distance to San Miguel, we never had to walk from Punta Gorda to San Antonio or any of the other posts. Unlike Andres Enriquez, my father had the benefit of a pension that he was able to survive on after his retirement before his passing thirteen years later, and he did not know the pain of losing any of his children or to be hospitalized with severe illness owing to the harsh conditions that he and his family had to endure.

Yes, so much has changed that it is hard to imagine the harsh realities that obtained in the past and the challenges pioneers of old had to face in building this nation. Today all our villages, including the newest ones in the Toledo District that has seen the greatest proliferation of villages in the country, are accessible by vehicular traffic. By 1964 when I was the teenage emergency principal of San Luis Rey School in San Antonio, Toledo, it was the largest rural school in the district with at least eight teachers. One-teacher schools are now a thing of the past. There are health centres within easy reach of practically all rural communities. Most have basic amenities like water supply and electrification. And there is access to secondary and tertiary education in each district. We have indeed come a long way, but it is important to be reminded that it was not always like this and that we owe a debt of gratitude to the unsung heroes, men, women, and their children who bore the brunt of the task of nation building, often at high cost to themselves and their loved ones. This book does just that.

This is a well written book, engaging and easy to read. I believe that for Jerry editing it had to have been a labour of love, as it is an important part of his own personal history. It is a rare, perhaps even a one of a kind, first-hand account of the service and accomplishments, triumphs and travails of Garifuna teachers and their families in rural Belize. It is an account of the critical role of women in this endeavour, a role that has never been given the prominence it truly deserves. And for me, it explains why Nurse Zenobia had the gift of healing and could have saved my baby sister from what otherwise would have been certain death. It explains why Solomon, Jerry's father, like all his other sibling could have been so proficient in all the languages spoken in Belize that there was a demand for them to serve as interpreters in court. It explains why my former colleague, Constantine, distinguished himself as a teacher following on the heels of his father and gave further exemplary service to the country as Education Officer. I also understand where Jerry got his social activism and strong commitment to social justice that extends beyond the Garifuna community. This is a must read for all those who are interested in Belizean history, nation building, education, culture contacts, and traditional medicine, among other things. You will not be disappointed.

E. Roy Cayetano, M.A.
Former Permanent Secretary,
Ministry of Rural Development and Culture

# *Preface*

Throughout my childhood years, my siblings and I enthusiastically listened to bits and pieces of stories that our father, Aunt Olive, and their siblings shared about their life experiences growing up in a number of remote Belizean villages where their father served as school principal. A few of their stories flowed with an aura of sadness; others were short bursts of memories to bring laughter at home and family gatherings.

But there was more to these stories that vividly demonstrated the uniquely rich connections that they had accumulated through the years. Family meals prepared by my grandmother and aunts were the most delicious combination of foods from every ethnic group they served in Belize. Every menu of Maya food, expertly prepared was a testimony of their immersion and service to the Maya communities of San Antonio and Crique Sarco. Likewise, the Mestizo foods showed evidence of their years of service in San Ignacio, Cayo District, and Progreso, Corozal District, while East Indian foods that my grandmother Jane Enriquez also prepared was learned during their work at TOPCO. Their own family ethnicity grounded them to Garifuna cuisine. Such diversity of cuisine also provided opportunities for historical discussions. Stories by my aunts about how they first learned to make corn tortillas and caldo, or about where they learned to make bollos and tamales provided more insights to the past.

Also punctuating the family's deep historical connections were the regular visits by various Maya individuals and families to our home in Punta Gorda. Some of these visitors came to seek my father's counsel on personal, family, or community matters. His communication with them in their own Maya language, his expert knowledge of their culture, and his educational background as a former school teacher all combined to provide his clients with unique depth of insights and charisma that they all admired. It was no wonder that he served as an interpreter of Maya at the Magistrate and Supreme Courts. As a child I saw several women visiting my grandmother's home for her massages, herbal medicines, counseling and midwifery services.

My father, Solomon E. Enriquez (1925-1986)

It was fascinating to see my grandmother, my father and his siblings, black Garifuna men and women, also expertly speaking English, Creole, Maya and Spanish—changing from one language to the other as the occasion arises. They even had recitations of prayers in Latin, a replica of those pre-Vatican II days when church services were conducted in that ancient language. Even within our home, we as children somehow knew that when the elders switched a conversation to Maya, it was because they were discussing something confidential. It was not uncommon for my parents and my aunts to welcome Maya, Garifuna and other visiting families from rural areas, numerous compadres and comadres, seeking an overnight lodging or a meal at our family home.

For about seven years from the early to late 1970s, an elderly single homeless Maya man, Mr. Telesforo Paquiul, the son of one of the founders of San Antonio Village, lived with our family at our home in Punta Gorda. That my father took in this octogenarian to live with us, showed remarkable compassion attesting to their long-standing family connection.

For my siblings and me, Mr. Paquiul became our adopted childhood grandfather. From him we heard numerous stories of his days in San Antonio. It was only after his health became too difficult to manage as he aged, that my father sought the intervention of Sister Cecelia's home in Belize City for his further care.

All of these childhood interactions and experiences at home deepened my awareness of the rich diverse historical experiences of my father's family. He and his siblings, and also my mother, Dativa V. Enriquez, were compadres and comadres to several Maya families. Later, as a young adult, I also stood in as compadre to a number of Maya families.

During a short visit to the village of San Antonio, Toledo, in the early 1990s, I encountered a simple, yet deeply profound, moment that would begin my quest for a deeper understanding about my family's connection there. This occurred at the home of Ms. Clara Bol, a family friend and former primary school student of my father when he taught in that village in the 1940s. While Ms. Clara and I were chit-chatting to share updates about our families, an elderly, shiny silver-haired, short, petit, Maya woman, probably in her 80s, neatly robed in her traditional dress stopped by and immediately set to inquire who I was. I didn't understand their brief discussion in their native language but the wide-eyed glow and enthusiastic whispered response of this serene elderly woman showed a feeling of surprise. Within three short slow measured steps, she stood in front of me joined her hands in prayerful position, closed her eyes with slightly bowed head, and uttered a few words in her native language.

"She is greeting and saying thanks to the spirit of your grandfather in you," was Ms. Clara's response as she translated what had just happened. The elderly woman repeated the gesture and left shortly after I expressed my gratitude.

Thus feeling deeply humbled, I probed Ms. Clara more about what she knew about my grandparents and family. That day strengthened my resolve to learn more about my family history through the experiences that the people of the community had with them. That would mean spending more time in San Antonio for interviews, and taking a pilgrimage walk from there to Punta Gorda through old forest trails was part of a plan I considered.

Within a few months after that encounter I finally decided to delve into old stored records and files of my father, who had passed away about seven years before while I was studying abroad. Among these were weather-beaten exercise books handwritten stories by both my grandfather, Andres Patricio Enriquez, and my grandmother, Jane Victoriana Enriquez. As if by some act of synchronicity, these writings appeared at a time when I was thirsting for some deeper understanding about their lives, to make sense of all the uniquely rich interactions and connections that I hardly saw in most other homes in Punta Gorda and across the country.

They both wrote their stories around 1950 just before my grandfather passed on. I believe that this was done not only to share their experiences and the broken-hearted disappointment they felt from discrimination by their employers after years of stellar service. Their stories might have been also written to appeal for support in their senior years after much family loss to hurricane, fire, and illnesses, since there was no pension scheme then. It was my father,

Solomon E. Enriquez, who started compiling his father's writing (which hardly required editing) as well as editing his mother's penciled handwriting. Unfortunately, due to weather damage, much of her work was lost, hence making her story seem abrupt and incomplete in this book.

One of the first persons to read the manuscript, a family friend Mrs. Pauline Williams-Sylvester, offered to carefully digitize each weathered page on her computer during those times when computers were not very common. Shortly thereafter, as his encouragement for me to publish these writings, Carlson Tuttle shared his amazing collection of historical notes and pictures that he had just unearthed from the Jesuit Archives. Numerous revisions followed in order to enhance the flow of the text and to place it in historical context. Accordingly, it was necessary to include historical information about Garifuna migration and settlement in Belize as well as that of the Catholic Church and its training of Garinagu leaders to spread this faith through the education system.

This autobiography by Andres and Jane Enriquez provide a uniquely personal glimpse of their family's experiences as they served to educate a number of remote communities throughout Belize. I am deeply honored and grateful that their lives have intricately weaved the fabric of who I am. I am also honored to pass on the torch of this foundation to my children, my siblings, other descendants of my grandparents, the broader public, and future generations. Their stories are also reflections of similar untold experiences now buried in the past of numerous Garifuna teachers who sacrificed their lives under most difficult challenges to educate a nation.

For those of us who have been born out of these experiences, we must always be reminded of this wise counsel by global spiritual leader Thich Nhat Hanh that, "If you look deeply into the palm of your hand, you will see your parents and all generations of your ancestors. All of them are alive in this moment. Each is present in your body. You are the continuation of each of these people."

I hope that readers will find something special and inspirational in these pages and that this book will prove useful within and outside our education system to build a greater awareness about Belize's history, especially the history of stalwart nation builders that is hardly known and increasingly lost in the national discourse.

Jeremy A. Enriquez<br>
August 2017

# *Acknowledgements*

I owe a debt of gratitude to a number of persons whose invaluable contributions and encouragement enhanced the completion of this autobiographical work.

First and foremost, I give thanks to my grandparents, Andres and Jane Enriquez, for sharing their reflections about their life journey. Although my grandfather passed long before I was born, and I only interacted with my grandmother during my early childhood, their life stories connected me in a special way to be deeply grateful for the tremendous sacrifices they made.

My childhood memories are filled with my grandmother's affectionate love and discipline. This autobiographical work of my grandparents provides only a glimpse of the immense personal sacrifices which they and many Garifuna teachers and their families endured as they worked diligently to set the foundations of education in rural communities all over Belize. Had they not handwritten their own personal experiences, which I found within their weathered old exercise book journals almost three decades later, much would have been lost to their descendants and others.

I am also deeply grateful to my father, the late Solomon Enriquez, for preserving their manuscripts with his collection of family memorabilia. As the eldest son of Solomon Enriquez, who is the eldest son of Andres Enriquez, who in turn is the eldest son of Joseph Enriquez, I feel eternally indebted and honored to be torch bearer of our family history to their descendants, just as they in their traditional Garifuna culture would have intended.

Since my childhood, the oral histories shared by my father and his siblings all grounded my awareness and connectedness to my roots. To all of them—my father, Solomon Enriquez, my aunts Olivia Hartman nee Enriquez, Zenobia Avila nee Enriquez and Elicia Enriquez, as well as my uncle Peter Enriquez (now all deceased) and Constantine Enriquez (the only surviving sibling)—I am eternally grateful.

My childhood and early adulthood interactions with my grandmother's siblings, namely, my granduncle Joseph Claro Villafranco, the youngest sibling, as well as my grandaunts Kate Villafranco Jimenez (a.k.a. Nitu Keta), Gertrude Villafranco Nunez (a.k.a. Nitu Bibi) and Barbara Villafranco Flores (a.k.a. Nitu Tu), now all deceased, all nurtured my deep appreciation for their life stories.

I gratefully acknowledge the insights I gained through historical discussions I had with my late uncles, first cousins of my father, Basilio Enriquez and Martin Alfred Enriquez, about their childhood experiences with their uncle, Andres Enriquez, who took charge of them after their father, Sylverius Enriquez, died at an early age.

Special thanks to Mrs. Pauline Williams-Sylvester who, in 1995, digitized the entire handwritten text from the original manuscript. I gratefully acknowledge the care and skill with which she deciphered the surviving text from weather-beaten brittle pages of the half-century-old exercise book. Many thanks also to Carlson Tuttle, genealogist and archivist of publications about Garinagu, and my cousin Andrew Enriquez for sharing their invaluable collection of historical photos and records.

I am particularly grateful for the persistent encouragement of my esteemed colleagues: Mr. Roy Cayetano, M.B.E. (retired Chief Executive Officer in the Ministry of Rural Development), and Dr. Joseph Palacio (retired Resident Tutor, UWI School for Continuing Studies)—themselves both sons of Garifuna teacher/families who lived in rural communities—as well as Mr. John Nunez, M.B.E. (senior lecturer at UB Toledo). Their wise counsel about the importance of sharing this example of the experiences of many Garifuna teachers and their families, helped to fuel the completion this book.

Finally, I give thanks to my wife, Cynthia Enriquez, for constantly reminding me of her eagerness to see in Belize's education system, a richer historical dialog that is inclusive of Belizean women's "her-stories", such as is revealed through this rarely-documented personal experience of our grandmother, a woman who stood strong to nurture and support her husband and their children as he served to educate a nation.

Jeremy A. Enriquez<br>February 2017

# Introduction

*"They tried to bury us. They didn't know we were seeds."*
— Mexican proverb

## Historical Background

The outstanding service of Garifuna teachers in spreading the Catholic faith and establishing the solid foundation of Catholic education in Belize has hardly been acknowledged in the country's documented history. Like buried pillars anchoring Belize's cathedrals to the subterranean bedrock of reclaimed Belizean swamps, the tremendous sacrifices of the Garinagu to teach in remote communities of Maya, Mestizo, Creole and others all over Belize have hardly been recognized.

For the most part, these teachers have left behind no literature or written tradition of any kind. Only occasionally are they remembered in isolated oral histories among their family members who know very well the hardships that they themselves endured in the remotest communities where their husbands, fathers, uncles or brothers and their families served. When their collective stories are heard, it must be conceded that there was no greater sacrificial service given by any other ethnic group in the early history of Belize, than the Garifuna teachers and their families who dedicated their lives to the education of other Belizeans in remote rural communities of pre-independent Belize.

## Garinagu Arrival and Settlement in Southern Belize

To understand why the Garinagu were chosen as key agents for Catholic evangelization and education, one must place in context their migration and settlement in Belize, and the critical role that they played in shaping Belize's economic, territorial and cultural history.

As a people whose reputation as sturdy workers made them both feared and sought after by European powers, the Garinagu became the primary agents for two of the most prevailing European interests during the early history of Belize:

1) the economic interest of the Belizean forestocracy to expand Belize's lucrative mahogany interests further south beyond what was then (in the late 1700s to early 1800s) the legally established Sibun River boundary, and
2) the interests of the English Province Jesuits with headquarters in Jamaica, then later the American Jesuits of the Missouri Province, to spread education in the Catholic faith to an increasing population of Catholics in Belize.

The Garinagu first migrated from Roatan (then a British settlement) to Belize in 1802, and perhaps some as early as 1799, to work in the lucrative woodcutting operations.[1] At that time, the Belize settlement was comprised of a total population of about 1,000 British inhabitants and their colored offspring, who were predominantly members of the Anglican faith, and about 3,000 enslaved Africans. Although the settlement was a "majority black society with an African rooted culture,"[2] its sociopolitical institutions and relations were dominated by oppressive British control such that from time to time the enslaved Africans revolted and escaped to neighboring Spanish territory.

By the time the Garinagu arrived, the major economic activity for the Belize settlement was the harvesting of mahogany for export, replacing logwood which had declined in demand since the 1770s when the use of synthetic dye became more popular. By the 1790s, virtually all the stands of mahogany within the territory north of the Sibun had been depleted.

In order to satisfy the steep demand for mahogany in Europe, the Belizean woodcutters sought to expand their operations south of the Sibun River, a territory that was then outside of Belize's boundary limits.[3] Emboldened by their resistance against Spanish invaders in September 1798, the settlers decided to ignore the established boundary of Belize and expanded their operations further south.

The white woodcutters' plan for expansion, however, was constrained by an increasing labor shortage resulting from the escape of brutally oppressed enslaved Africans to the Yucatán in Mexico and in the Peten area of Guatemala, as well as to the territory south of the Sibun River. Although enslaved Africans comprised seventy-five percent of the population of the settlement in the 1790s, these escapes were made "with such regularity and in such numbers that their masters often felt that the very existence of the settlement was threatened by this phenomenon."[4]

Given these frequent and heavy losses of enslaved Africans, the woodcutters needed all the labor they could get.[5] Only five years earlier in 1797, the rebellious Garinagu had been forcibly exiled *en masse* from their homeland island of St. Vincent to Roatan, after their unsuccessful battle to defend their native territory against invasion by the British superpower. Soon after, they made themselves well known in the region for their intelligence, independence, fierceness and hard work. Consequently, they became eagerly sought after as labourers in the British woodworks.[6]

With some government assistance, about 150 Garifuna persons were shipped to the settlement of Belize, the first shipment being in August 1802 and another in December of that year. In the following years, many more managed to find their way to the southern coast of what became the Stann Creek and Toledo Districts.[7] This early and subsequent influx of the Garinagu to Belize provided a major boost in the pool of labor to expand the operations and economic benefits for the Belizean woodcutters.

Although their labor was greatly valued, the Garinagu were at first considered dangerous and were suspected of cannibalism, treachery, and savagery. There was fear amongst the English settlers in Belize Town that the Garinagu, as free Blacks who were well known for the fierce war they had led at St. Vincent only a few years earlier, could pose considerable danger of leading an insurrection. After all, the English settlers would not have forgotten the numerous slave revolts which had occurred in the settlement during the mid to late 1700s.

On December 17, 1802, Mr. A. Cunningham of the settlement reported to the magistrates that he "sees great danger in the presence in the settlement of numerous Caribs, he believes the number to be 150, stating that everyone is aware of the atrocities committed by these people in St. Vincent and points out that with Christmas approaching, when the brains of the best servants will be inflamed with liquor, the dangers of insurrection led by these people will be considerable." Furthermore, he requested "that the Magistrates hold a special meeting and consider the propriety of expelling these people from the settlement."[8]

Even though the Garinagu were forbidden from living among the enslaved Africans in the settlement, there was still suspicion among the ruling class about the propriety of their visits to Belize Town. In part due to the Anglo-French wars between 1803 and 1814, and news about the Haitian revolution around the same time, the English residents of Belize suspected that the Garinagu, one of the first free Afrodescendant people in the hemisphere, were not completely loyal to them.

Because of these suspicions, tighter restrictions were imposed on the nature of work done by Garifuna persons, their association with the enslaved Africans, and on visits by any Garifuna person to the settlement. To further ensure that no secret associations were made between the enslaved Africans and the free Garinagu, the magistrates also decided on August 29, 1806, to prohibit the enslaved Africans from playing Gumbay drums or holding nocturnal meetings after 9 p.m. In October of that same year, one of the enslaved was sentenced to 39 lashes for playing the Gumbay after 9 pm.

At another Magistrates meeting held on March 16, 1807, the Superintendent stated his surprise to find that, "in spite of his warnings that all Caribs must be viewed with suspicion, Caribs have been sent to man the lookout post on Cay Corker, which is one of the highest importance." Consequently, he arranged to send out the Government boat the next morning "to fetch them in" with the trust that the magistrates "will find trustworthy men to replace them."[9]

On July 11, 1811, the High Constable was directed to warn all Caribs "who could not produce a permit or ticket from the Superintendent, to quit the settlement in 48 hours ... or subject themselves to imprisonment ... as the Magistrates consider them a most dangerous people."[9]

On July 16, 1811, a few days after the decree, those Garifuna persons who had been imprisoned, were ordered to be "sent away in any of their country craft as early as possible by the High Constable."[10] On July 6, 1812, "a hefty fine of fifty pounds sterling was set for anyone who hired or employed in Belize, any Carib."[11] Since the Garifuna people lived outside the then jurisdiction of Belize, the affluent and influential merchants and woodcutters ignored the injunction and continued to clandestinely hire them.

As a result of these concerns, the Garinagu established their own settlements south of the Sibun River where almost all of their communities, such as Dangriga, Hopkins, Seine Bight, Punta Gorda, Barranco and others, have remained ever since.

The first group of Garinagu who settled in Stann Creek (now Dangriga) later proved to be "an exceedingly friendly, reliable, honest people" though considered to be "addicted to polygamy and obeah superstitions."[12] Their skill in expertly speaking three or more languages was also admired. Because of their prior history with the British and French in St. Vincent, the British in Roatan, and the Spanish on the Honduras mainland, many of them were able to speak all three European languages besides their native Garifuna language. There was very little crime or violence and the ill-feelings they harboured against the British had been restrained as they focused on their economic survival. They proved to be so industrious and "well-behaved" that others were subsequently admitted.[13]

The year 1823, marked another major influx of Garinagu who came seeking refuge from the interminable civil wars, assassination attempts and revolutions that preoccupied the Central American republics around that time. This migration of Garinagu to Belize occurred about ten years before the emancipation of enslaved people throughout the British Empire was declared on August 1, 1834. A few years before, in 1820, there was a major armed revolt by the enslaved, which took place on the Belize and Sibun Rivers. By that time, however, Garinagu communities were strictly confined south of the settlement.

Garifuna family in front of home in Punta Gorda in the early 1900s.

For decades, the eager, hardworking and skilled Garifuna woodcutters penetrated the forests south of the Sibun River all the way to the Sarstoon River, which became formally recognized as the southern boundary of Belize in the Treaty of 1859. In those early years, Garifuna women and children also occasionally accompanied the men to the lumber camps.[14] As for the Garifuna women, their primary productive work was in agriculture. It was they who produced much of the foodstuffs, chickens and pigs for sale in Belize. By the mid 1800s they were also employed in bagging and stacking cohune nuts. Later when bananas became an important export, some men joined the women in establishing plantations.

Garifuna men also became well known for their excellent maritime skills. Their skillful maneuvering of their small boats and their intimate knowledge of the entire southern coastline made them prime smugglers in the area. As such they commanded the respect of merchants and citizenry as well as the exasperation of government authorities.

Over decades, the tough rigors of their work in forestry, their strong maritime culture, their harsh history of battle against European powers and subsequent expulsion, their Catholic background, as well as their productivity, natural intelligence, facility for language, and resilience had all molded among the Garinagu the pioneering spirit and work ethic that made them and their descendants be considered as prime candidates for establishing schools in the remotest areas of Belize.

### *Foundation of the Catholic Church in southern Belize*

Catholic missionary work in southern Belize began around the early 1830s, about two decades before the church was formally established nationwide in 1851. Around 1832, Fray Antonio, a Franciscan priest from Honduras had been ministering to refugees from Honduras who had settled in the Mullins River area.[15] Around that time Fray Antonio also served the few Catholics of the Belize settlement who were mainly merchants from neighbouring republics conducting business in Belize, which was at that time a main trading entry point for all of Central America. Fray Antonio returned to Honduras in 1836 and was replaced by Fr. Rubio from Bacalar. The first Belizean Catholic Church was built in Mullins River from where other Yucatecan priests then ministered to the Catholics of the south.

*Introduction* 7

Between 1847 and 1855, following the Caste War in Yucatan, Mexico, thousands of predominantly Catholic Spanish and Mestizo refugees fled to settle in northern Belize. In response to requests for priests by this new Catholic population, the Vicar Apostolic of Jamaica, Rev. Benito Fernandez O.S.F. traveled to Belize accompanied by Fr. Eustace Du Peyron, S.J., to formally establish the Belize Mission. By December of 1851, Fr. Du Peyron oversaw the construction of Belize's first Catholic Church, the Church of the Most Holy Redeemer, which was completed in 1853.

Within a few years thereafter, the Jesuits expanded their mission and formally established parishes along the entire coast of Belize. In 1859, the Corozal parish was established to serve the Catholics originally from Yucatan, and in 1862 and 1867 respectively, the Punta Gorda and Dangriga parishes were established to serve the predominantly Garifuna Catholic populations in those communities. Thus, the foundation stone for the new Catholic mission in Belize was officially laid.

Prior to 1812, there was no place of worship in Belize although the settlement had been inhabited for well over a century. Formally established in 1812 as the first church in Belize, the Anglican Church made no effort to extend its reach beyond Belize Town or to evangelize and integrate the Garifuna and Maya settlers of the south or the Mestizo settlers of the north, as that church seemed to have been established mainly to serve the white settlers and their colored offspring.

The Baptist Church was built in 1822; the Methodist Church in 1825; and in 1850, the Presbyterian Church. There were no schools in the Settlement around that time. Only the privileged few owned books. The Methodist Church faced many challenges in their attempts at evangelizing in Dangriga and failed to attract large congregations as many Garinagu refused to abandon their traditional practices or their allegiance to their Catholic background.

By the early 1900s, within a little over half century of its establishment, the Catholic Church in Belize absorbed the majority of Garinagu, Mestizo, and Maya populations and rapidly grew from being virtually non-existent and unknown to representing 60 percent of Belize's entire population.

Although they strongly guarded their traditional spirituality, the Garinagu who came to Belize were primarily considered to be

This Catholic Church in Punta Gorda, built in 1892, was dismantled and replaced in 1970. Top shows church view from the sea, including the rectory and the pier from which the priests travel to coastal communities. Bottom shows the church.

Front Street, along the coast of Punta Gorda before the 1945 hurricane.

Front Street, Punta Gorda, 1936

Front Street Punta Gorda in 1921

at least nominal members of the Roman Catholic faith, having been previously evangelized by zealous Spanish priests in Honduras, and to a limited extent, if any, by the French missionaries they encountered in their original homeland of St. Vincent prior to their violent expulsion by the British in 1797. Those who first settled Punta Gorda were among the first seeds from which the Roman Catholic Church in Belize was formally established.

The earliest date recorded in which a Catholic priest conducted missionary work in Punta Gorda was 1841,[16] nearly two decades before that part of the territory far south of the Sibun River border was formally incorporated as part of Belize.[17] In May 1845, the Roman Catholic Church established a small mission in Punta Gorda.[18]

The Jesuits who had ministered there reported that the Garinagu had retained many of the old Spanish Catholic customs and were reciting their prayers only in Castilian Spanish.[19] By that time, Punta Gorda was already a well-established Garifuna community. In 1842, John Stephens, a U. S. visitor, described Punta Gorda as a community which, "consisted of about five hundred inhabitants. … Besides cotton and rice, the cahoon, banana, coconut, pineapple, orange, lemon, and plantain with many other fruits which we did not know even by name, were growing with such luxuriance that at first their fragrance was oppressive."[20]

Around 1859, the Garinagu of Punta Gorda also began to receive intermittent missionary visits from the Jesuits of the English Province who had been stationed in Belize Town from 1853, under the jurisdiction of the Vicar Apostolic of Jamaica. Names of priests like Fathers John H. Genon, Salvador di Pietro (who later became the first Vicar Apostolic of British Honduras in 1893), Aloysius Pozzi and Alphons Parisi fill up many pages of the baptismal registers in Punta Gorda.[21]

After the Punta Gorda Parish was established in 1862, its first resident priest was Fr. John H. Genon, S.J., an esteemed Belgian priest who was first based in the Garinagu community of Livingston, Guatemala, before moving to take residence in Punta Gorda. Fr. Genon's plan was to unite the widely scattered Garifuna population of the coasts of Honduras, Guatemala, and British Honduras into one separate ecclesiastical Mission with its headquarters in Punta Gorda. In order to bring this about, he returned to Belgium to recruit priests and nuns to return with him to Punta Gorda. Of all the nuns he recruited, only one made it to Punta Gorda.

Fr. Genon lived among the Garinagu for more than twenty-five years, sailing up and down the coast from Livingston in Guatemala to Stann Creek (now Dangriga), or even to Belize City. So as not to burden the people with his maintenance, he cultivated his own small plantation of cassava and plantain in Punta Gorda and each morning after Mass he set out in a dory to fish for himself and to share with others who were sick.

Fr. Genon's attempt at creating a special Mission for the Garinagu, however, proved abortive because of internal difficulties experienced by the missioners he had recruited from Belgium and the complexities involved in uniting three distinct political territories under a single ecclesiastical jurisdiction, especially during the times of political instability in the Central American republics.

The group of zealous Belgians whom he brought to Punta Gorda for this cross-border Garifuna mission stayed for only a few months as they had become, "worn out by hunger and fevers produced by the poor shelter afforded by the huts in which they lived."[22] Consequently, one of the priests was transferred to Belize City and another, Fr. Lootjens, who became very proficient in Garifuna, was transferred to Stann Creek, while Fr. D'Hont remained in Punta Gorda with Fr. Genon. There he worked diligently but he never recovered his health and died within the year. The only nun who was part of that group was transferred to Jamaica but the fever had broken her health and within a year she died.[23] Thus ended the special mission for the Garifuna.

In 1871, when Father Joseph Woollett, S. J., Pro-Vicar-Apostolic of Jamaica, came to visit the Mission, he ordered the Jesuit residence in Punta Gorda closed because of the extreme poverty of the congregation. In 1874, the residence was re-opened after a more commodious church and residence were built, and Fr. Genon was again placed in charge. Fr. Genon continued to work alone among the Garinagu of Punta Gorda until his death in 1878. Punta Gorda has remained a permanent Jesuit residence ever since.

During those years of its establishment in Belize, the view of the Catholic church about the Garinagu can be glimpsed through numerous reports by its missionaries. One such view can be found in a report by Vicar Apostolic, Fr. Woollett, S. J. following his visit to Belize in 1873. In that report he compared the Garifuna people to the then recent descendants of Maroons and formerly enslaved Africans in Jamaica, noting that, "These Caribs for the most part understand Spanish, but they understand English still better than Spanish. I believe all the Fathers have this opinion, and certainly I met some Caribs who understood me speaking in English better than a Father who spoke in Spanish. But now, these Caribs have certainly formed themselves into a distinct people along this south coast of British Honduras as the Maroons in the mountains of Jamaica have formed themselves as a distinct people, from a mixture of the blood of different nations." Fr. Woollett concluded that in comparison to the descendants of enslaved Africans, he generally found the Garifuna, like the Maroons, to be of superior intellect.[24]

Another priest, Fr. Eugene Brady, in a letter about his visit to Belize in 1895 reported that the natives were, "too clannish to approve of hospitals and orphan asylums. They care for their own sick, and for sick relatives, and though destitute of most of the comforts of life, they personally care for the sick neighbor. If parents die, the children are assimilated in some neighboring family; and the orphan simply changes its home."[25]

Following his visit to Stann Creek Father Di Pietro comments on the work of Father Brindisi "in civilizing them, building church, house, and school, and the improvement of this people. But unfortunately they are falling back; they have no more such great respect and interest for the religion and the priests. ... One of these is a kind of devilish dance that they call "mafia." It is an old national ball that they were accustomed to dance when pagans... and which they kept in spite of all the efforts of the missioners to destroy it."[26]

A Jesuit report in the 1890s described the Garifuna as people who are "fine mahogany cutters and, being in fact amphibious, they are splendid sailors. Their dories may capsize and their effects be lost, but they are never lost (so is the saying), as they can swim any length of time. ... It is very odd, however, that the women do all the agriculture, in fact all the work except wood-cutting and seafaring. The husband takes his ax and clears a piece of ground, and his work is done; the wife or daughter then begins her task, planting corn or cassava or yam or pines, tends the growing crop and gathers it in its season. To the women, of course, falls all the work of the household, whereas the men begin their genteel life even in their boyish days. .. But since the schools have been spread they have done remarkably well, and will compete with any boy of their standard in the colony."[27]

Other descriptions in missionary records described the Garifuna as, "in many respects the most interesting of our peoples. They are a black, stalwart, well-proportioned people, thrifty almost to miserliness, very stubborn and stiff of character, and hard to impress: once however they have been won over, they are very faithful. They have certain deep-rooted objections to marriage, based upon long-standing custom—much preferring a sort of 'Scotch marriage.' But even in that regard they are improving wonderfully. In six years their pastors have blessed 365 marriages, really a great number for the number of souls. But it was no easy task. Preaching seemed to have little or no effect; there must needs be individual exhortation."[28]

As shown in the 1881 census of British Honduras, the total number of Garifuna (then referred to as Carib) was 2,037 or seven percent of the country's total population of 27,452. Creoles (or "Colored and Blacks" as stated in the census) numbered 12,148, or 44 percent, while the Mestizos (referred then as the "Spanish Element") numbered 12,157 or 44 percent of the total population.[29] Of the country's total population of 27,452, an estimated 20,000 or 73% were Catholics.[30]

The Catholic school in Punta Gorda must have been established during the period of Fr. Genon's residence in that community. When Fr. Genon returned from Europe to recruit priests and nuns he also brought his nephew who became the parish gardener and likely assisted the nun as a school teacher. This nephew also served as caretaker for the Punta Gorda mission while it was closed. From the years 1884 to 1888 Fr. Parisi, S. J., was reported as the head teacher of the school in Punta Gorda and he was assisted by Miss Isabella Warwick.[31]

In 1887, school returns from Punta Gorda reported a total of 72 students, 56 boys and 16 girls. The priest in charge was Rev. Joseph Piemonte, S.J.[32] By then, Garifuna men were already being trained as pupil teachers and eventually became principals of the schools in Punta Gorda, Barranco, and other rural areas.

In 1888, the Punta Gorda school had its first Garifuna Head Teacher, Cirilo Gutierrez, who later served as a teacher in the Barranco school from 1894-1896. One Mr. Arzu was the Head Teacher in Barranco in 1892.[33] By the time Punta Gorda was officially declared a town on January 21st, 1895, the church and school were well established.

Other head teachers at the Punta Gorda Catholic School include Secundino Ogaldez, Remigio Marin in 1893, Antonio Enriquez in 1903, and Secundino Ogaldez again from 1904 to 1908, Justino Ortiz from 1909 to 1913, and Marcelino Arzu from 1915 to 1918. The longest serving Garifuna head teacher at the time was S. B. Daniels, who served from 1919 to 1931, before the school was handed over to the Pallotine nuns to manage from 1932 to the mid-1970s.[34]

The number of Catholics in southern Belize received a significant boost by the influx of near 800 Mayas into rural Toledo District from the village of San Luis in Peten Guatemala around the 1880s. Wearied by the oppressive and cruel conditions meted out to them by Guatemalan government officials, the Mayas escaped across the border and placed themselves under the protection of the British flag.

Since these new migrants were considered nominally Catholics, Fr. Parisi who had been working in Punta Gorda initiated work on evangelizing them. To reach them, he traveled the rugged journey inland on foot and by dory up the Temash and Sarstoon Rivers. Around the early 1890s, Fr. Piemonte also worked among the Mayas of San Antonio Village and Sarstoon. He focused not only on their spiritual affairs but also took care of their temporal needs, by begging clothes for them, assisting them in building their huts and cultivating their plantations while teaching them the Catholic faith. Fr. Parisi, Fr. Piemonte and other Jesuits also began establishing schools in these Maya communities.

The Catholic church in Punta Gorda was originally called St. Michael the Archangel Church. Later it was renamed St. Peter Claver, in honor of that Spanish Jesuit who was canonized by the Pope Leo XIII in January, 1888, for dedicating his life to the primary needs of the often sick and broken slaves who arrived in the early 1600s on the shores of Cartegena, in present-day Columbia, South America. The official renaming ceremony of the church occurred on Sunday, September 9, 1888, the Feast Day of St. Peter Claver. On that day, after a preliminary two-day celebration, the statue of St. Peter Claver, also declared a celestial patron of all Negroes, was set up on the main alter of the church in Punta Gorda. Thus, the parish, together with all Garinagu were placed under the protection of this saint.

Father Joseph Piemonte, who had served there as pastor for many years, directed the solemn procession along the primitive streets of the town with the statue of the "Slave of the Negroes," while the Superior of the Mission, Salvador di Pietro, S.J., was present to act as celebrant at the Solemn Benediction of the Blessed Sacrament at the close of the procession.

Since its formal establishment in Belize in 1851, the Roman Catholic church grew to become the predominant faith among the Garinagu in southern Belize, as well as among the Maya and Mestizo populations and to some extent the Creole population throughout the country.

By 1910, there were 635 Catholic Garifuna in Punta Gorda and another 215 in the village of Barranco. In addition to Barranco there were twenty-one other rural stations attached to Punta Gorda, some of them taking a journey of three days by sea and river to get there in missionary dugout canoes.

At the same time, 2151 children were attending the Catholic public schools of Belize. Additionally there were St. Catherine's Academy under the Sisters of Mercy with 125 students enrolled, and the younger St. John's College, the successor to a school that was previously established by the English Jesuits.[34] Around the same period, of the 3,000 persons in Dangriga, then the second largest town in Belize, near 2,000 were Catholics, under the care of Fathers Cooney and Lynam.

In the early 1950s, after it was recognized that the ancient Garifuna language had not been written, Father John Stochl, S.J. organized a group of his Garifuna students at St. John's College to study the language and establish a Garifuna writing system. This SJC Carib Language Group included Augustine Flores, Eugene Hernandez, Govel Morgan, Clifford Palacio and Theodore Palacio, as well as Martin Avila and Osmond Peter Martin who were both studying at Kenrick Seminary in St. Louis. After months of hard work and valuable assistance provided by older folks like Candido Arzu, an alphabet and spelling system was developed and the first English-Garifuna dictionary was published. Prayers, hymns and stories were translated and words that were almost forgotten were recalled. The publication of the *Carib-English Reader* by Martin and Avila in 1952, was the first of its kind by native-born Garifuna.[35]

## Role of Garifuna Teachers in Catholic Education in Belize

While the Garinagu are now highly acclaimed for their dominant musical and cultural impact in defining Belize's image at home and abroad, it must not be forgotten that it was their dedicated work, in partnership with the Jesuits, that established the solid educational foundation for building Belize. They were well known to "provide many of the best school teachers in the colony."[36] From the 1880s to the 1970s, Garifuna men were trained and deployed by the Jesuits as teachers/catechists to spread education and the faith to rural communities all over Belize. Primary education was the tool used to facilitate indoctrination into the Catholic faith.

To be employed as teachers in these hinterland communities these men had to possess a reasonably solid and above-average education, qualities of leadership, good character, a pioneering spirit, physical and mental stamina, and adaptability to survive harsh, rugged life in these remote settings.[37] In those days, Garifuna men were also recognized by the Jesuits to possess a natural ability to teach. They were also admired for their mental aptitude and willingness to learn different languages.[38]

Although the salary of teachers was very low, their standard of living was relatively above that of their other peers who were usually fishermen, tradesmen or laborers. The respect accorded

Garifuna teachers in front of St. Peter Claver Parish Hall in Punta Gorda, May 1936
Andres P. Enriquez, 12th from right. His nephew, Basilio Enriquez, 6th from left.

to those in the teaching profession gave them a certain degree of standing in the community. For decades up to the 1950s there was no pension for these teachers to receive after their retirement. It was only after the 1950s when communities became more accessible by road, that women were employed to teach in rural areas.

For many years, the Punta Gorda Mission was the only source of Garifuna teachers for schools all over the country. A number of them were pupil teachers or former students from St. Peter Claver R. C. School there.

Although the training of pupil teachers began as far back as the 1880s with such priests as Fr. Averbeck, it was Fr. Tenk who was most involved in teacher training at a large scale. Fr. Tenk served in Punta Gorda for almost twenty five years (1913-1937) He worked hard to give these teachers every advantage during their training to become both efficient teachers and men of superb Catholic character. Apart from teaching in urban schools, Garifuna teachers have taught in virtually every rural Catholic school in every district all over Belize. These include schools in Aguacate, Baking Pot, Barranco, Benque Viejo, Bermudian Landing, Blackman Eddie, Bullet Tree Falls, Caledonia, Carmelita, Caye Caulker, Chunox, Crique Sarco, Cristo Rey, Douglas, Forest Home, Guinea Grass, Hopkins, Maskall, Monkey River, Mullins River, Newtown, Patchakan, Progreso, Roaring Creek, San Antonio Cayo, San Antonio Toledo, San Estevan, San Jose, San Narciso, San Pedro Ambergris Caye, San Pedro Columbia, Sarteneja, Seine Bight, Succotz, Teakettle, Xaibe, and Yo Creek.

Fr. HermanTenk served in Punta Gorda from 1913-1937, the longest serving priest in Punta Gorda

## Andres Patricio Enriquez (1886-1951)

My late grandfather, Andres Patricio Enriquez was conferred M.B.E. (Member of Order of the British Empire) by His Majesty the King George VI for his over 45 years of outstanding service as a teacher in the then colony of British Honduras. His experiences provide a glimpse of what other Garifuna teachers and their families experienced. Born on November 10, 1886, in Punta Gorda, he attended the Catholic school there from around 1891 to 1899 and was also taught by one of the early Garifuna teachers, Secundino Ogaldez, who was stationed at the school from 1890-1893. His uncle Antonio Enriquez, who was a head teacher at the school in 1903, might have also influenced him to join the teaching profession.

Andres Enriquez was the eldest of three children born to Joseph Victoriano Enriquez and Maria Genara Colindrez. His only brother was Sylverius Enriquez and his only sister, the youngest child, was Rosenda Enriquez. With both of his parents deceased by the time he was 12 years old, young Andres and his siblings were taken under the care of his aunt Juliana Colindrez, also known as Da Blackie for her darker-than-usual skin color. After he completed primary school at age 14, he was trained as a pupil teacher by the school manager Fr. Averbeck, S. J.  He was also trained by Secundino Ogaldez, who was again the Head Teacher of St. Peter Claver School from 1904-1908. There, and occasionally in Barranco, Andres Enriquez served as pupil teacher, and later class teacher, for about 4 to 6 years.

Andres Enriquez served in San Antonio, Toledo District, for many years in multiple roles as Head Teacher, community leader, counselor, and catechist. It was he who successfully reopened the school in 1907 after it had been closed several times since its opening in the late 1890s. Before him, other teachers had made several unsuccessful attempts to keep the San Antonio school open. Their attempts failed due to lack of interest on the part of the parents to send their children to school, and the extremely harsh living conditions that those teachers could not accept.

The determination of Andres Enriquez to remain steadfastly as the principal over several years was critical for the stability needed to develop the school and the community. Andres Enriquez worked and lived in San Antonio for a total of 28 years in two periods, 1907-1917 and 1932-1949, and was the longest serving Head Teacher of that village. He served in a similar capacity in San

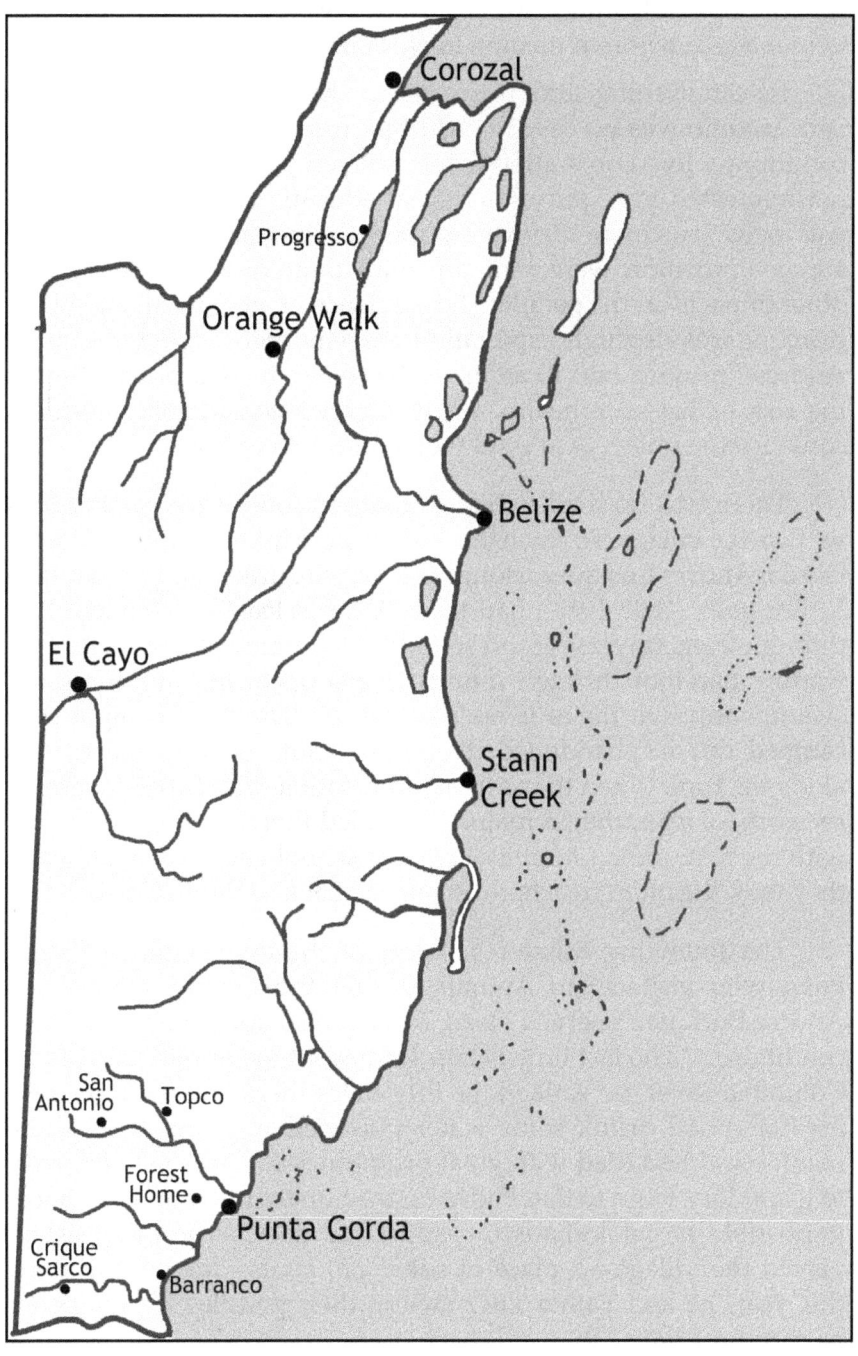

Map of Belize showing rivers, towns, and locations where Andres Enriquez served as Head Teacher.

Ignacio (1918-21) Progresso (1921-28), Forest Home, Barranco and Crique Sarco before returning to work in San Antonio.

Re-establishing and maintaining the school and church in San Antonio was no easy feat. At that time, Maya families of that community lived on scattered and isolated plots of land, and were not interested in acquiring a formal education. Life in the village was focused on mere survival from subsistence agriculture. Poverty and malnutrition were rampant with their resulting health and other impacts on the people. The incidence of alcoholism and binge drinking was also high, especially among the men of the community. Andres Enriquez had to adjust to these harsh conditions, often at the risk of his own health, while exerting considerable effort to convince the villagers to send their children to school.

There was no road to San Antonio in those early years of his work in the village. To reach that village from his hometown of Punta Gorda, Andres Enriquez, along with his wife, my grandmother Jane V. Enriquez (1895-1968), had to walk for at least a day and a half through trails traversing forest and hills for almost 25 miles, often wading barefoot through muddy, waist-deep, mosquito-infested swamps through the area now known as "Dump." At night they camped out in abandoned dilapidated huts of logwood cutters along the trail. When they arrived in the village at the beginning of each school year, they remained secluded there, having no contact with the rest of their families until the school vacation break when they took the often treacherous journey back to Punta Gorda.

The following Mission's report of the experience of Father Fusz, who visited San Antonio during those early years when Andres Enriquez's served Head Teacher also aptly described these conditions: "The last time Father Fusz went to San Antonio on the Columbia River, he walked the fifty miles there and back, because his horse had drunk some water poisoned with the juice of the manioc and had died with great promptness. ... It is not very easy to get a dory to go to San Pedro on the Sarstoon River, and almost impossible to get Indians to paddle the dory. When the Bishop visited the village—a place of some 250 souls—for the first time this year, he and Father Fusz swung their paddles for the better part of three days."[39]

In the village Andres and Jane Enriquez had to make do with living in the huts designated as teachers' quarters. Due to the harsh, sacrificial living conditions that they persistently endured in San

Antonio, none of their first five children were born alive. Around 1930, while he served as Head Teacher at Forest Home, they also lost their two-year-old child, Equitius, when an influenza epidemic that ravaged through the community and other parts of the country, also afflicted their entire family.

The travel to coastal or riverside communities was no less treacherous. To reach Crique Sarco, they and their young children, along with their luggage, were loaded into narrow canoes with boatmen paddling upstream against the strong currents of the Temash River to reach their station. When they could afford to go home for school vacations, they traveled with their children all the way from Progresso in the Corozal District, where they were stationed for eight years (1921-29), to Punta Gorda. The journey from Belize City to Punta Gorda usually took overnight on often rough seas.

In San Antonio and Crique Sarco, where Andres Enriquez served, Jane Enriquez had to wash in the river, carry buckets of water for home use each day from the well or river, and cook over an open fire hearth. In various communities where they served, they both had to learn the native language as they adjusted to the new culture.

In Barranco, they stayed in a teachers' quarters infested by vampire bats that sucked their children even under nets, until they learned the local ways of repelling the bats. If their family got ill in such secluded areas, they had to concoct their own healing remedies.

The expenses of the teacher and his family's travel to and from various stations, and for transfer to other stations came out of their own meager salaries. During those earlier days, there was also no pension, no social security, nothing to fall back on after years of service. Upon retirement in their old age, teachers were left to fend for themselves and their families.

It was only when Andres Enriquez worked in hospitable communities, such as San Ignacio or Progresso, or when Jane Enriquez briefly remained in Punta Gorda to give birth, that seven children were born alive: Olivia, Zenobia, Elicia, Solomon, Peter Equitius, and Constantine. Except for Equitius whose life was taken by influenza at age two, these children spent most of their childhood and young adult years in San Antonio.

Like their father, Olivia, Solomon, Peter and Constantine became teachers in various rural schools across the country. Constantine, now the only surviving child, retired as an Education Officer in the Ministry of Education, migrated to live abroad for a few years, and then returned to Belize City where he currently resides.

Like her aunt Pastora, the youngest sister of her mother Jane, Zenobia became a nurse. Like the families of other Garifuna teachers, the family of Andres and Jane Enriquez, including all their children, were very articulate in Garifuna, Maya Mopan, Spanish, and English, a powerful nation-building skill that was hardly ventured or attained by other ethnic groups in Belize.

Since the priests visited the village about once every three to six months, Andres Enriquez, like the other teachers, also held over as the catechist to sustain and nurture the Catholic faith. In between the periodic visits of the priests, he conducted prayer services, Sunday services, funeral services, and taught the faith as he resided among the people.

It was only after the Punta Gorda-San Antonio Road was completed in 1940 that the church built a residence to accommodate the priests. The attractive stone structure of the new presbytery was far more durable and comfortable than the harsh native conditions under which the teacher and his family lived for decades. These comforts provided for foreign priests and nuns were not made available for local teachers.

Jane Enriquez became a well-known mid-wife and traditional healer in San Antonio several years before the health center and nurses' quarters were built there in 1947. While living in San Antonio, she developed her traditional healing skills. There she delivered many babies and many from the community depended on her for healing and counseling. In Punta Gorda she was also well known for her traditional healing services.

The stories written by themselves in the following pages, provide a glimpse of their own experiences during their years of service in education of rural communities in Belize.

### *Other Outstanding Garifuna Teachers*

Experiences such as these portray only a glimpse of the personal and family sacrifices that several Garifuna men and their families have made in their service as pioneering partners in taking education to the remotest areas all over Belize. Among these outstanding men were Cyrillo Gutierrez, Secundino Ogaldez, Eugene Cayetano (the father of Roy Cayetano, retired CEO in the Ministry of Rural Development), John Zuniga (the father of Edmund Zuniga, retired Auditor General), Charles Martinez Sr. (father of former Area Representatives, Charles Martinez Jr. and Peter Eden Martinez), Francis Cayetano (the father of Rev. Callistus Cayetano, and his brothers Joseph, Fabian, Sebastian, and Alfonso), Simeon Marcus Sampson Sr. (father of Simeon Sampson, Jr., an outstanding lawyer in Belize), Santiago Labriel, who served in Punta Gorda from 1913 to 1937, (grandfather of former National Garifuna Council President Ernest Castro), John Paulino, Aparicio Marin, Sam B. Daniels, Francis Martinez, Peter Avila, Joe Ogaldez, Candido Arzu, Theodore Palacio, Cyrilo Arana, Godsman Ellis, Octavio Castillo, Leonel Perez, James Lopez, among others too numerous to mention. Just as they maintained superb character, they expected and demanded no less from their families and the communities where they served.

## Impacts of Garifuna Teachers on the Development of the Catholic Church

It is not surprising that, as a natural progression of the foundations laid by their ancestors, a number of Garifuna men became priests, including Fr. Callistus Cayetano, Fr. Marin, Fr. Lloyd Lopez, Fr. Lazarus Augustine, Fr. Larry Nicascio and others. The late Bishop O. P. Martin, formerly a Garifuna teacher, became the first Belizean Roman Catholic Bishop. Succeeding him, Bishop Larry Nicasio became the third Belizean and second Garifuna Roman Catholic Bishop in Belize. A number of Garifuna women became nuns, including Sr. Barbara Flores, Sr. Irene Locario, Sr. Mary Avila, OSP, Sr. Josita Marie Ogaldez, Sr. Mary Julia Apolonio OSP, Sr. Joan Flores, Sr. Evelyn Estrada, Sr. Josita Ogaldez, Sr. Esther Marie Estero, Sr. Mary Rebecca Carlos Castillo and Sr. Jean Martinez, among others.

While the descendants of the British and Creoles, who were mainly of the Anglican or Methodist faith, saw and guarded their upward mobility mainly through the colonial and postcolonial public service, the Garinagu in those days saw theirs mainly through teaching and their commitment to the church. Many who further qualified themselves in professions apart from teaching often faced discrimination within the public service such that they and their families were left with no other choice but to migrate to the United States or work in foreign-owned companies or

Top: San Antonio Church, 1900s. Fr Fusz is in the middle
Bottom: San Antonio stone church and presbytery (*right*) in 2017

organizations where their character and service tended to be far more valued.

Ironically, as the brightest and the best Garifuna leaders were deployed to serve other people and other communities throughout the length and breadth of Belize over several decades, this brain drain has arguably diluted the likely powerful development impact on their own Garifuna communities to result in the impoverished and vulnerable socioeconomic conditions that these communities face today. The challenge now is for Garinagu to honor the legacy of their forebears and continue through their various professions, to build strong foundations upon which more people can benefit.

—Jeremy A. Enriquez
February 2017

## Endnotes

1 Gonzalez, Nancie L., 1988. *Sojourners of the Caribbean: Ethnogenesis and Ethnohistory of the Garifuna*. University of Illinois Press: Chicag, p. 54.
2 Shoman, Assad, 1994. *A History of Belize in 13 Chapters*. Belize: The Angelus Press, p. 24.
3 The Convention of London of 1786 established the territory limits of Belize from the Rio Hondo to the Sibun River.
4 Shoman, 1994. p. 36.
5 The Abolition of Slavery Act was only put into force in Belize on August 1, 1834. The final installment of Emancipation came four years later in 1838 with the Abolition of "Apprenticed" labour.
6 Caiger, Stephen L.,1951. *British Honduras: Past and Present*. London: George Allen and Unwin, p. 110.
7 *Ibid*. p. 110.
8 Burdon, Sir John Alden, 1934. *Archives of British Honduras*, Vol. 2., from 1801-1840. London: Sifton, Praed & Co.
9 *Ibid*.
10 Gonzalez, 1988, p. 56.
11 *Ibid*.
12 Caiger, 1951, p. 110.
13 *Ibid*., p. 110.
14 *Ibid*., p. 134.
15 Hopkins, Frederick C. The Catholic Church in British Honduras (1851-1918): *The Catholic Historical Review*, Vol. 4, No. 3 (Oct., 1918), pp. 304-314. Catholic University of America Press <jstor.org/stable/25011583> Accessed, Dec. 10, 2016.
16 Quirinus P. Leonard, S. J. Meet the Black Caribs in *Jesuit Missions* Vol XII, No. 9, October pp. 236, 251-2.
17 The 1859 Anglo Guatemalan treaty formally established the Sarstoon River as the southern border of Belize. Prior to that, Belize's border was the Sibun River above which was illegal for the Garinagu to settle. When the Garinagu first came to Belize in 1802 to seek employment in the logging operations, they settled south of the Sibun River in the area not yet declared as part of Belize. (Metzgen, Sigfrid M. and Henry Edney Conrad Cain. 1925. *The*

*Handbook of British Honduras.* London: The West India Committee, p. 12.).
18 Quirinus P. Leonard. S. J. "Meet the Black Caribs" in *Jesuit Missions* Vol XII (9) October pp 236, 251-2.
19 Shoman, 2011.
20 *Ibid.*, p.18.
21 Brixtow, Lindsay W. & Philip B. Wright, 1888. *Handbook of British Honduras, 1888-89.* Edinburg & London: William Blackwood & Sons.
22 Richard Buhler, S.J., 1976. A History of the Catholic Church in Belize. *Belize Institute for Social Research and Action.*
23 *Ibid.*, p. 18.
24 A. M. D. G. *Letters and Notices* March, 1873.
25 Our Trip to Belize, British Honduras. A Letter from Father Eugene H. Brady to the Editor, *Woodstock Letters,* Volume XXIV, Number 2, 1 May 1895.
26 A. M. D. G. Letters and Notices Vol. XIII. Letter from Father S. Di Pietro to Father Provincial dated July 30, 1880.
27 *Woodstock Letters,* Volume XIX, Number 1, 1 February 1890.
28 *Woodstock Letters,* Volume XXXIX, Number 3, 1 October 1910.
29 A. H. Anderson, 1958. *Brief Sketch of British Honduras.*
30 Our Trip to Belize, British Honduras. A Letter from Father Eugene H. Brady to the Editor, *Woodstock Letters,* Volume XXIV, Number 2, 1 May 1895.
31 Carlson Tuttle, personal communication.
32 Brixtow, Lindsay W. & Philip B. Wright, 1888. *Handbook of British Honduras 1888-1889: Comprising Historical & General Information Concerning the Colony.* Edinburgh & London: William Blackwood & Sons.
33 Carlson Tuttle, personal communication.
34 Personal communication from Peter L. Enriquez from his notes from Jesuit Archives.
35 Clifford J. Palacio. St. John's College Experience. <slideshare.net/MyrtleP/experiences-at-st-johns-college-under-the0jesuits>.
36 The Mission in British Honduras. *Woodstock Letters,* Volume XXXIX, Number 3, 1 October 1910.
37 Quirinus P. Leonard, S.J. Thank you, Father Tenk: An Appreciation, in *Jesuit Bulletin*, Feb 1965.
38 *Ibid.*
39 *Woodstock Letters,* Volume XXXIX, Number 3, 1 October 1910

## *Au le, Andres Patricio Enriquez**

Way back in the year 1907, in Punta Gorda my hometown, there was stationed a good old priest named Fr. Henry G. Huerman S.J. (of saintly memory) who was in charge of the rural missions in the district.

On a certain day that year Antonio A. Avila, a good friend of mine, informed me that the Reverend Fr. Huerman was seeking for a teacher to reopen the school at San Antonio, Toledo District. That school, which was established around the 1890s, had only functioned off and on until it was finally closed down in 1905 due to the lack of interest on the part of the parents to send their children to school and the considerable hardships that teachers had to bear. All those teachers who had been posted there had stopped working within a few months. This time the church, in its determination to re-open and sustain the school and mission in San Antonio, wanted a teacher who was also committed to this undertaking.

As I had just given up my career as a pupil teacher after about four years at the Catholic School in my above-mentioned hometown, and as the opportunity offered itself, I immediately tendered an application for the post, hit or miss. That was in the month of June 1907.

Imagine the foolish daring of a twenty-year-old young man to attempt to undertake such a position in a Maya community. In those early days the Maya lived a sort of primitive, semi-nomadic life deep in the forest and moved from one area to another as they pleased in search of new lands. Part of the mission of the church was to have the Mayas live a more settled life in a community in order to more effectively meet their spiritual and education needs.

Only about two decades earlier, in the 1880s, San Antonio was settled by a group of about one hundred Mayas who had fled their

---

* *"Au le"* means "I" as spoken by the Garifuna male

Andres and Jane Enriquez and family, July 12, 1928
(*children from left*) Olivia, Elicia, Peter (baby),
Zenobia, and Solomon

village of San Luis, Peten, Guatemala, to avoid further cruel and brutal treatment meted out to them at the hands of officials and subordinates of the Guatemalan government. During those years, the Mayas were always compelled to some form of service for the government. This included carrying loads of provisions over distances that took about two months to travel and return to their homes. They were also forced to carry rocks like beasts of burden to various sites for building roads through the forests of Peten.

As conditions worsened, the leaders of the community made secret plans to evacuate their people to the neighbouring country of British Honduras and establish a village where they could live in peace and comfort. On a certain night, parties of the population began their exodus across the border in a journey that took several days.

At first they settled for some months in San Antonio Viejo, now Pueblo Viejo, but being near the border Guatemalan soldiers and officers invaded and harassed them, claiming that they were still within their territory. Consequently, the people decided to move further inland to Aguacate to rid themselves of further disturbance from the Guatemalans. Dissatisfied with the fertility of the soil there, the leaders sent another party to find a new place for the wandering people of San Luis to finally establish a settlement.

When the expedition party returned with the glad news of their discovery of an area with rich fertile lands and creeks flowing perpetually, most of the people packed up their belongings and moved to settle in the community now known as San Antonio.

The church wasted no time in seeking to establish a mission among this new population, considered to be nominal Catholics, in the remotest part of the district, then inaccessible from Punta Gorda.

Before I arrived, the church had not been successful in keeping the school open. There was some resistance by the people to settle in one place. They were also quite isolated from others outside of their group and were unaccustomed to the world outside their immediate surroundings. The goal of the church was to educate and convert them.

My application to teach in San Antonio was accepted but it was not until August of that year that I received the orders to go up to the station. Rev. Franciseus J. Kemphues, S.J. (of saintly

School Principal, Mr. John Zuniga teaching a class lesson at a rural school, Toledo District, circa 1960s.

memory), who was the assistant pastor at Punta Gorda, was sent along with me so that he would make the necessary arrangements for my maintenance and have me officially installed.

What a treacherous journey it was! Because of the rainy season, the trail of about twenty-five miles was in the worst condition for traveling. Fr. Kemphues rode on horseback but could have only done so for about five miles from Punta Gorda. Horses could not travel further up the trail then, due to its most horrible condition with mud, puddles of water, large swamps, and fallen trees. While he rode for the first part of the journey, I had to travel the whole distance from Punta Gorda to San Antonio on foot.

It took us two days to cover the distance. The first night we camped at Condemn Branch Settlement, a distance of about ten to eleven miles from Punta Gorda. Bad as the trail was on the first day, it became indescribably worse the following day. There were countless numbers of tree stumps and roots along the trail. There were also large pools of water, swamps and veritable quagmires, and all had to be crossed.

Early the next morning we resumed our journey. The reverend gentleman put on a pair of oilcloth pants to protect himself from the water and mud. I wore nothing but underclothing as I trudged barefooted through the swamp. Crique Piedra was flooded to its highest level. It was a veritable lagoon about a mile long right across the middle of the trail. There was a primitive kind of ferry in the water, called "balsa," and we traveled on that for a part of the lagoon. We waded through the rest of the way until we got to the mud swamp. This swamp was a mile of real quagmire where one sank to his thigh at almost every step he made.

Just think for yourself how much fear and regrets crept into my heart in the midst of such a jungle of forest as it was then. We finally reached San Antonio at around six in evening of that second day, Saturday.

At a meeting convened by the priest the following morning, the villagers agreed that all able-bodied persons of the village should contribute towards my maintenance until better living conditions were arranged.

For my living quarters, I was offered a small bare thatched hut with earthen floor; its walls were made of sticks tied closely together. My bed was a hammock. My personal belongings were meager. It consisted of the bare necessities from the luggage that I brought on my back from Punta Gorda. It was in that hut that I would retire in solitary confinement after each day of hard work at school and the community, far away from my family and my people. It was there on many dark nights that I often reflected and planned how best to fulfill the mission at hand.

My salary then was only a pittance of eight dollars a month, although in my case no monthly payments were made to me until I could collect the total sum when I returned to Punta Gorda for vacation months later. For my sustenance, I had to make do with whatever the community offered to support me and whatever I could find in the village. The school was still a private church school, as yet not government funded.

During the first few months after my arrival, I had the misfortune of boarding at the home of the First Alcalde, Jose Oh. Although he made a public commitment at a village meeting to provide for my meals, his wife Felipa Oh, who did the cooking, was a most termagant woman. She scolded, grumbled, swore and all the rest of it the whole day long. Only put yourself in my place, and imagine how you would feel when each time you go for meals you meet with a grumbling, swearing and insulting woman. As was agreed, this woman served my meals. However, she was not consistent in preparing meals and only did so when she pleased. Otherwise she prepared nothing but corn tortillas and pepper and served me with the greatest contempt.

Soon I began to get from others, hints to the effect that the woman was also railing and grumbling to them all the time about my having meals at her home. Although it was her husband who had arranged that I should board at their home, she was one of those who were most opposed to having a school in the village. She also did not like the idea of having any outsiders there. Moreover, her husband committed her to a task that she did not want.

Because no alternative arrangements could have been made for my meals during those first months, and I was at a distance that seemed like a continent away from home, I had to muster the greatest patience while I ate. With each difficult bite of food I swallowed my pride. Many were the days, on dark lonely nights, that I lay in my hammock regretting with bitter tears ever taking up such a job under such arrangements. As a result of the poor diet, I became undernourished and gradually lost my former good health.

Along with the other hardships of living in that village, it was these types of insults as I received from Mrs. Oh and other villagers that had caused previous teachers to abandon their efforts and close the school. However, I had promised the priest that I would not give up easily and would remain determined through the challenges of re-establishing this school.

Only three paltry dollars were advanced to me by the manager before I started. Out of that I sometimes helped the kitchen out with fifteen or twenty-five cents. Think of this grand initial advance at my disposal to go and start such an undertaking among a people widely scattered throughout the forest in the area.

During school time I had to make strenuous sacrifices to motivate the children to attend classes regularly, to stay in school, to understand lessons being taught in a language that was new to them. The children also had to adjust to learning from a new person who hardly knew their language. Furthermore, it did not help that there was strong resistance from several parents who preferred to have their children stay at home to work there or at their plantations.

The parents also had to be convinced. Each weekend I would take time to visit various families to talk with them about the importance of school for the development of their children and their community. At community meetings or prayer services that I held, I would also encourage the parents to send and keep their children in school. I started the school with about forty children of all elementary school ages.

All these challenges — my boarding arrangement, primitive living conditions, isolation and loneliness, declining health, resistant parents, and adjusting to a new culture — were terribly difficult for me, but I was determined to endure this one day at a time. Feeling rather lonely when my twenty-first birthday came on November 12th, 1907, I knelt down early that morning in my hut before I began my day's activities, and prayed for good fruits to come out of my labor and sacrifices.

After a few months, I finally told the Alcalde that I had enough and demanded a change from his home. My health was getting worse due to the poor diet that I was being served. Arrangements were quickly made for me to transfer to another family — the home of the Deputy Alcalde, Tranquilino Chen. His wife Luciana Chen did the cooking and I must confess that after all my hardships with Felipa, the first cook, Luciana was a veritable ministering angel to me. One could feel her caring efforts to make me eat well within their limited dietary options. Even the surroundings for eating in their smoky, thatched, mud-floor kitchen were far better. She and her husband went out of their way to make sure that my meals were adequate. During that time, the school received a government grant and my salary was raised to $13.75 per month.

I remained at my new boarding quarters for quite some time. Since I was then beginning to get a little money more regularly, I was able to maintain myself with other foodstuff that I would bring back from Punta Gorda when I returned from visits there during the school holidays. Once in a while whenever I had some spare time on Saturdays, I visited Tranquilino's plantation and assisted him with his work there. The crops that he planted provided his family meals. I always remember the kind hospitality that Luciana and Tranquilino accorded me at their fireside.

During my first year in the village, I also met the elders and personal leaders who were involved in the migration of the people from San Luis, in the Peten District of Guatemala. These leaders related to me their own personal experiences of leading the exodus of their people from Guatemala into the territory of British Honduras to settle first in Pueblo Viejo, then Aguacate, and finally San Antonio. These gentlemen, now deceased, are Jose Maria Paquiul, Benito Tzucanal, Manuel Cho, Leonardo Yacab, Felipe Cho, and Francisco Tesecum.

Fr. E. Courtney. S.J., giving cathecism lessons to Maya villagers in San Antonio, 1935

Time went on more or less tolerably and through my interactions with the villagers, especially at the fireside in their homes, I learned the Maya language.

Part of my duties as the teacher was also to serve as the cathecist in the community. This means I had to conduct prayer and burial services and to teach the doctrines of the church since no resident priests were there at the time. I am indebted and bow my head in obeisance and gratitude to Mr. Secundino Ogaldez and the Rev. Aloysious Averbeck, S.J. who were my teachers as a boy and as a pupil teacher at St. Peter Claver School. Consequently, I credit whatever good I may have done in my teaching career to them.

Fr. Aloyius Averbeck, S.J.
Served Punta Gorda in 1896 and 1899-1903

Fr. Louis J. Fusz
served Punta Gorda 1908-14

From time to time, about once every three or four months, travelling missionaries visited San Antonio. A few of the notable ones were Reverend Fathers, A. Averbeck, S. J., who had been a teacher of mine when I was a pupil teacher, C. M. Charroppin, S.J., and Louis J. Fusz, S.J., all of whom have passed on to their reward. During these visits, the priests performed baptisms, marriages, confessions, and masses. In between their visits I also prepared the students for their first Holy Communion and for Confirmation.

Religious instruction was a daily part of the school curriculum and church hymns were taught in both Latin and Maya. Occasionally the bishop made his visits to administer the sacrament of Confirmation to the young people. Church services were held in the new metal roof church building that was built in 1906, the year before I arrived. The former thatched church that was built around 1896 was destroyed by fire.

In June 1912, during my school vacation in my hometown Punta Gorda, I got married to my wife, Jane V. Enriquez. Immediately thereafter I took her to live with me in San Antonio. She was a very great consolation to me after four years and nine months of solitary, lonely life in this very remote village.

But alas, think of the struggles she encountered as she adjusted to living a very remote area and in a culture that was very different from ours. At first, she found the people quite strange. As a young woman, 16 years of age, who was leaving home for the first time, she had to get used to the different food, customs, language and all the differences that she experienced in the new culture and place. The adjustment to all these new experiences caused some hardships for some time until, after much encouragement from myself and through the friendship she gradually developed with members of the community, she learned to accept the living conditions and way of life there.

At that time it was still impossible to get our provisions from Punta Gorda, and so on very many days our diet was only corn tortillas spiced with a mix of pepper and lard. We did not know the taste of sugar for weeks, for the natives could do without it and did not care to make rapadura, their native sugar, when they ran out of sugar.

I must not forget to mention that the first five of our children, the fruits of our marriage, were all stillborn. This could have been caused by nothing else but the severe strain that my dear wife had to bear in the village or whenever she traveled down to Punta Gorda to give birth. There was no convenient place for giving birth in the village, nor were there any competent midwives in the area.

Furthermore, so as not to interrupt the school days we could only leave the community for the vacation break at Christmas or the end of the school year. The rugged journey of twenty-five miles from San Antonio to Punta Gorda was a great strain for a pregnant mother to walk. Even when we took the journey by dory through the Conejo route by river and often rough sea after walking from San Antonio to Conejo, it was still a strain. Those long hours of sitting in a narrow dugout canoe and sleeping overnight in makeshift camps alongside the river bank as we traveled to Punta Gorda were difficult and risky for my wife as it would for any young mother, especially during her late stages of pregnancy. Under such conditions, none of our first five children were born alive.

On one occasion, in December 1913, I became very disappointed and annoyed at the people's lack of concern and insensitivity to my wife's condition. We were about to travel down to Punta Gorda that month for the school vacation, as was our custom. Because of my wife's pregnant condition, I made an agreement with some Maya men to carry our luggage to Punta Gorda.

However, for some reason or another they reneged on their agreement on the day of our scheduled departure. No matter how hard we pleaded or tried to cajole, explaining that with my wife's condition we really needed their assistance, they refused for no other reason than they didn't feel like doing any work that day or the other. In my wife's condition, staying in the village was a risk. Although walking to Punta Gorda was also a risk, we felt that it would be better to be with family members around this time. There were also good midwives among our people.

In the end, my wife and I, feeling very disappointed, had to walk the journey on our own. We each carried our own luggage as we trudged the two-day journey through the hilly and muddy jungle trails to Punta Gorda. Along the way we made several rest stops as I wanted to ensure that she was not taking too much strain. A few days after we arrived in Punta Gorda, however, my wife had a miscarriage. We both felt very sad.

That miscarriage made me very annoyed at the Maya men's behavior. I was even more disappointed when I kept wondering why they would do this despite all the sacrifices I had made for their community and their children. While their children were benefitting from the sacrifices that my wife and I were making for their education, we were losing ours. As a result, I refused to return to the village in January 1914 to reopen the school after the Christmas vacation. The school remained closed as I remained in Punta Gorda to start a plantation and did some fishing to support my wife and myself.

For those seven months that I remained at home, the priest met me several times, persistently trying to persuade me to return to reopen the school. He explained that since I had already set up a good foundation for the school, and since I had begun to establish good relations with the people, knowing their language and culture so well, it would be difficult to find a replacement at that time. Furthermore, he explained that sending a new teacher at that time would be like starting all over again, especially after previous attempts with the teachers before me had failed.

Eventually my wife and I decided to try again. I returned after the outbreak of World War 1 in August 1914, and stayed there until 1917 when I was transferred to the Forest Home School while I fully recuperated from an illness that year. The strenuous work and living conditions in San Antonio were taking its toll on my body.

During the time that I worked at San Antonio, the school population was steadily increasing. At the time of my departure there were about one hundred and twenty five pupils, up from forty pupils when I first started. Because of the presence of the school and church, San Antonio and its residents began to remain more stable. Before this, the people migrated a great deal from one area to the next wherever they found good land for their plantation. Naturally, they also took their children out of school to go along with them. It took a great deal of effort on my part and on the part of the mission to convince the people to remain settled and to have their children attend and stay in school.

The school at Forest Home Village was in its infancy then, and I labored there for some months before being transferred to Barranco for a brief period. From Barranco, I went back again to work in Forest Home in 1919.

No child of ours was born alive until 1918, the year after my wife and I left San Antonio. Olivia Justiniana Enriquez, our first child born alive, was born in Punta Gorda on September 5, 1918.

In June 1919, an appointment reached me to take up the post as Head Teacher at El Cayo R.C. School and I accepted it. All went well there. The members of the teaching staff were Miss Irene Smith and Miss Juana Requena and the school manager was Fr. Huerman, S.J. The school had about 150 children. Around that time, Mr. Salvatore B. Daniels had just succeeded Mr. Marcelino Arzu as the teacher in charge of the school in Punta Gorda, and one Mrs. Baldwin was a teacher there. In Barranco, the principal was Mr. Simeon M. Sampson while Mr. S. Avilez served as pupil teacher there that same year.

In June 1921, only two years after my family and I had settled so well in El Cayo, my peace of mind was broken by the news that I received of another transfer. This time it was to Progresso, Corozal District. This transfer was being done to make room for the nuns who were to take over the school when it reopened after the holidays. By the time I was leaving, the building where my family and I stayed was being renovated and expanded to accommodate the nuns.

At Progresso I gave eight consecutive years of my classroom experience to the most grateful, friendly and appreciative community ever known to me in my entire teaching career. Parental co-operation with the teacher was the most outstanding character of the people there at the time.

However, in the midst of this acceptance and appreciation that I cherished from the community, I continued to feel a deep inner longing to return home to Punta Gorda or to work nearer to home. With three of our children born at Progresso, our family had then increased to five children. This increase was making it more expensive to travel back to Punta Gorda during vacation. I was afraid that with the escalating cost of travel from the northernmost part of the country to the southernmost town, my family might one day not be able to afford to return to the rest of our family. Neither could we communicate as often as we would like especially in times of emergency. There were times that close family members in Punta Gorda died and we would not hear until weeks after.

These concerns particularly nagged me after my wife, children and I suffered a number of illnesses at Progresso. Although we had wonderful support from genuinely kind and considerate friends in the community, I could not resist the call for returning home. When it overcame me, I placed an application for a transfer.

In June 1929, I was sent again to Barranco. I found that there was a lot more work to be done to improve the discipline and academic standards of the pupils. I made extra effort to give them additional lessons and eventually I saw much improvement. What I found most challenging was the living conditions that my family and I had to cope with. The house we stayed in was bat-infested and dilapidated. Since there was no other alternative to be found we had to adjust as best as we could.

Quite often, parents were not enthusiastic in their support of activities relating to the school and this was discouraging especially seeing this among my people. This, along with the harsh living conditions, made our stay more challenging. Dissatisfied and disappointed at the lack of cooperation and at a wild uproar started by some of the parents at a school entertainment that I was staging there one night, I was determined to get out of the village as soon as possible. After the positive experiences I had with the parents of the schools at El Cayo and Progresso, it was difficult to deal with the behavior that was displayed by some of the parents in Barranco.

The following year, in August 1930, my transfer was made to TOPCO (Tropical Oil Products Company) Estate, to establish the school there. At TOPCO I experienced great sadness at the sufferings of one of my children. The child had a sore on her foot, and relying on the flat car (that was the only traffic there) to take us up to the camp from the landing, I arranged for my family to come up on a certain day. But alas, the disappointment! The car left us and we had to do the rest of the eleven-mile journey on foot as well as we could.

We had not even reached half way when night overtook us. By now the sore-foot child was tired and my wife and I had to take turns to carry her on our backs. About halfway through the journey to Camp One, both of us were so tired of walking knee-deep in the mud, and my poor daughter with sore foot was so broken down with pain, that we had to get a lodging place for all of our other four children to spend the night. Only my wife with the youngest baby and I proceeded the rest of our journey of eight miles through the mud to our station. We reached there very late at night. Imagine how we were feeling then, having started at 4:30 p.m. The four children, including our daughter with sore feet whom we had left behind at Camp One, reached us the following day, all looking miserable and haggard—a veritable picture of misery and bitter suffering.

It was at TOPCO that a very sad affliction befell us; our then youngest boy, Equitius, became very ill and died. He was buried there. Other troubles we also experienced were my family's overcrowding in a little room we had for a home and the bad quality of water we had to use for drinking. There, in May 1931, four members of my family fell very sick at the same time: my wife, two of our three boys and two of our three girls. After long and patient waiting for a means of transportation, we decided that the sick ones would be taken down on mule backs to the landing now called "Cattle Landing." There they spent two nights before being transported to Punta Gorda in a motorboat. It was the most pitiable sight to see these sick members of my family landing on the public pier at Punta Gorda.

After 15 months of service at TOPCO, I was transferred to Crique Sarco on the Temash River, in January 1932. The place was so remote and unattractive that I longed and yearned to get out

Garifuna Teachers at a Catechist Training Retreat in Punta Gorda, taken in May 1936 in front of St. Peter Claver Church. The teachers are numbered with circles above and to the right: 1) Fr. Robert J. McCormack, S. J., 2) John Zuniga, 3) Eugene P. Cayetano, 4) Andres P. Enriquez, 5) Candido Arzu 6) Basilio Enriquez, 7) Simeon M. Sampson Sr., 8) Santiago Labriel, 9) Santos Arzu, 10) Francis Cayetano, 11) Joe Ogaldez, 12) Anthony Lewis, 13) Sam B. Daniels, 14) Felix Noralez, 15) John Paulino, 16) Peter Avila Sr., 17) Ben Hector Contreras, 18) Francis B. Martinez (*numbers above and to the right of the indicated person*)

of there as soon as possible. I stayed there with my family from January to April that year.

In June 1932, the natives of San Antonio wrote a petition to the then school manager begging that I be sent back to them. Since I left there in 1917, at least six teachers in succession were stationed there but had to quit for one reason or another. Only one of them had held out for four years.

I was reluctant to go at first, but the offers and promises made to me were so enticing that my reluctance gave way and I agreed to try again. All went well at first. When the day came for me to go up, men from the village came to Punta Gorda with seven horses to take up my whole family — six children besides my wife and me — and we enjoyed a splendid time on the trip. Fine!

Up to December of that year was an uneventful period, save a little misunderstanding here and there with the school management and the people. It was my custom in those days to go down to Punta Gorda to spend the Christmas holidays and return to reopen school in January, but because traveling with six children was becoming more difficult and impracticable, this had to be discontinued.

One May, I arranged a trip for the family to go down to Punta Gorda town to spend the summer vacation there. At the appointed time, one of the natives explained that he would guide us through a better trail in order to avoid the hilly and difficult swampy parts of the usual road.

We started our journey very early that day, but had not traveled very far when I began to regret having gone through that trail. It was fairly dry indeed but the hills were so steep and the trail was so near the edge of the top of the slope that I expected at every moment to see someone of our number fall off a horseback into the valley far down below. Such a fear came over me on those hills that I did not speak even a single word until at long last we reached the flat, thank goodness, without any mishap. Having reached there, traveling became easier and more bearable.

At a certain point on the road, however, our horses got too close to each other. Among them were two stallions that began to fight each other in such a way that my poor little girl riding one of them was thrown off to the ground. One of her feet got under the hoof of one of the beasts. While I held the rest of the animals as best as possible, I simply was at a loss to do anything at the moment. My wife, seeing the danger, jumped off her horse as quickly as possible, got in between the two beasts and saved our girl. Fortunately the injury was only slight and after applying some medicine and exchanging horses to keep the stallions apart, we proceeded. So terrified were we that my wife and I uttered not a word until several minutes after.

My first real conflict with the people of San Antonio began when a man named Sabino Sho died. Everyone knew that Sabino had been living an openly scandalous life of adultery up to the time of his death. As was the custom then, the teacher would pray over the dead at church before the funeral. Knowing that my superiors would dislike the idea, I explained the situation to the village leaders and refused to pray over Sabino's body. As a result, a group of about twenty men entered the school building where I was, and tried to intimidate me into submission to their desire. They threatened to harm me violently with their machetes. Seeing that I remained calm and was unmoved as I stared directly at them, they all went away and left me in peace — even those who had attempted to assault me. Just look at that! All was pacifiable.

The first resident priest that was installed in San Antonio was the late Rev. Allan A. Stevenson, S.J., who arrived there for

Fr. Allan Stevenson in a dory with Maya guides. Fr. Stevenson was also known as the missionary dentist for the Colony; he extracted thousands of teeth.

that purpose in 1942. He did not last two years, for sickness and ill health undermined him until he passed away in 1945, in the United States.

My real troubles at San Antonio began just after the freak hurricane of October 1945 that severely damaged the entire Toledo district and resulted in tremendous losses suffered by my family. Not only did we lose all our belongings in San Antonio, but our home in Punta Gorda, like most of the others there, was also severely damaged. Although the material loss was severe for us, we were thankful that none of our family members, relatives and friends lost their lives. Fortunately also, except for one elderly woman who we heard was killed by a fallen tree, there was no other loss of life anywhere from the hurricane. Our family had to lodge temporarily in one of the classrooms while our house was being rebuilt.

Along with the stress of our losses, the serious troubles that came immediately following the hurricane were the conflicts being generated in the village by a priest and the newly stationed police officer of Creole descent who developed an apparent racist hatred toward me.

Soon after he arrived at the station in San Antonio, this officer grew envious of my family's strong influence among the people after I tried to advise him to show more respect in his relations and approach to them. As a result, he started to spread mean and false rumors about me, trying in every way to undermine my integrity. Along with a few villagers he plotted for my removal from the village.

Not long after the policeman arrived, another priest was also sent to be stationed there. Both the priest and the police officer became great friends and unfortunately the priest and the policeman colluded against me. This priest was also envious of the close relationship the natives and my family had developed. With myself having worked and lived among the villagers for twenty-eight years, not only as a head teacher but also helping in that role to keep the village stable from the people's otherwise nomadic existence, there were no other persons than our family with whom the villagers built such strong trust and confidence. The people confided many of their problems, struggles and sensitive information to me and members of my family. Apparently our popularity and role in the village made the policeman and this particular priest very uncomfortable. They both knew that the people told me about some unacceptable behavior that they displayed. Quite a number of times I had to intervene on behalf of the people who at times felt threatened and bullied by them for no apparent reason.

My interventions only caused more tension between these men and me. As a result both of these newcomers tried very hard to instigate the people to break their attachment to me. They also advised, and when they failed, demanded, that the people no longer ask me to be their compadre for baptism, confirmation or marriage as they used to do. When I confronted the priest about this accusation, he denied it saying that he only wanted the natives to be more independent of outside assistance.

Try as he did to discredit me, no success crowned his efforts. That priest was eventually transferred, and two others, one after the other succeeded him for some months each. Fortunately these two priests were peace loving and men of Christian principles.

As bad as the first resident priest had been, the one who replaced him after the two temporary ones, was doubly worse for he arrived with evident hatred for me, and everything that pertained to me. Apparently influenced by the first priest, this other priest treated me with evident revenge and contempt, and schemed and made all possible efforts to degrade me. He even openly asked the villagers not to support me in any way because I was not of their race.

This situation occurred while there were widespread concerns among the villagers about some unusual behavior that they had been observing of that priest. I believe the missionary was very uncomfortable to know that the villagers were confidentially sharing these concerns with me. As a result our discussions usually became tense as he often tried to treat me in a condescending manner.

Matters got to a head, one day, when in a discussion I calmly commented about the contrast between the modern structure and living facilities of the newly built presbytery and that of the Principal and his family. I questioned why it was that the Principal who had sacrificed and labored so hard in this community for so many years, even before that priest was born, continued to live in native thatched huts, while everything was being done to make the priest live so comfortably. Even after the hurricane destroyed all our belongings no effort was made by the mission to improve the housing conditions for the teacher.

This practice occurred in many of the larger communities. Whenever the priests or nuns went to reside in a community, all efforts were made to make them live comfortably. This includes the construction of spacious, comfortable houses for them, while the local teachers who spent years in the community and sacrificed so much of themselves and their families, were forced to live in very degrading conditions. Furthermore as soon as the priests and nuns settled in those communities, the local teacher and his family would be pushed to another remote community to struggle again under similar degrading living conditions. This practice was noticed in Punta Gorda when the nuns first arrived there, and at Fairview where the local teacher was transferred from there all the way to San Pedro Columbia to accommodate the nuns. At El Cayo, my family and I were pushed out to Progresso while urgent repairs were done to make way for the nuns. The case in San Antonio was quite similar.

When the resident priest arrived, it seemed as though he felt very uncomfortable with the complete confidence that the people had in me. Consequently, he wanted me to be replaced by someone quite unfamiliar with the village so that he could establish his own power over the villagers without any question or challenge.

This particular priest continued his attempts to instigate some villagers to go against me, and when he failed, he made false reports in the strongest terms that my performance at the school was very poor, and made recommendations that another person should be the principal. Naturally, the mission's head office in Belize City believed the reports of this priest, as the word of a fellow priest, without question, carried weight over any native.

During that brief period of conflict that I experienced in the village, a fire of questionable origin totally destroyed the house where my family and I were staying. Just as we were recovering from the loss of the hurricane, we lost hundreds of dollars in property that were accumulated over years and could not afford to replace most of them.

Soon after the fire, the priest served me with a notice in January that I should resign from teaching. No reason whatsoever was given. When I made representation about the unfairness of the matter to the head office, they kept me in suspense by their temporizing without any reply.

In the last week of February 1948, when I went to collect my month's salary at the mission, I was informed rather bluntly that as from the reopening of school, I would no longer serve at the school and that my service was terminated. I went home to my family feeling shocked, disappointed and dejected that a priest could have instigated such division and hatred after my 28 years of fully dedicated service to that village. Moreover, the losses from the 1945 hurricane, the total losses from the fire, the tense divisions created in village and then the sudden termination of my job all happening within a short period of time in my older years, made me very sad.

As time went on, I reported my situation to the Department of Education and also to the Federation of Teachers. These bodies took up the matter seriously and vigorously. It was quite clear to them that my termination was wrongful. By an order from the Director of Education, John W. Forrest, the termination was rescinded and an order was given that I be reinstated. Later, the Catholic management notified me about a transfer, not termination as they had first decided.

Getting back my teaching job in June 1949, however, was a blessing and a curse. Instead of being posted in Punta Gorda or another nearby school, the church authorities banished me to San Antonio in the Cayo District, one of the most inaccessible parts of the Colony, with no all-weather road for transportation by vehicles. I believe that this was done out of spite especially at my later age and after more than four decades of dedicated service I have given to the teaching profession in rural areas all over the colony. Having suffered the loss of everything my family owned and with no pension to receive after years of service, I had no other choice but to accept.

I was sent to San Antonio, Cayo, as the Principal to succeed Lauriano Garcia, another Garifuna teacher originally from Seine Bight. My wife, two of my young adult daughters—Olivia and Elicia—and my youngest son Constantine accompanied me.

The journey from San Antonio Toledo to San Antonio Cayo proved to be the longest, most hazardous and grueling ordeal I had ever undergone in my later years. First we had to travel by chartered truck with the remainder of our family belongings from San Antonio, Toledo to Punta Gorda. After a few days in Punta Gorda we took the regular overnight journey to Belize City by sea on the boat, Heron H. From Belize City we traveled on a truck for the seventy-two mile rough bumpy trip to El Cayo. For the final part of the journey rough, bumpy ride from El Cayo to San Antonio, Cayo, the local manager surprisingly offered to take us. Accordingly we all squeezed into his jeep with as much luggage as possible.

The eight mile distance to San Antonio was so rugged that it felt like more than double its distance. The dark, hilly, muddy road caused the jeep to slide off the track so many times, causing the mud to splatter all over us. Because of the condition of the road, the trip which would have otherwise taken half hour at most, took about three hours. We arrived in the village after nine o'clock that night, all muddy and exhausted. The rest of our luggage remained in El Cayo and was brought by the local manager within a day or two.

For the most part San Antonio, Cayo, was accessible only by horseback from El Cayo along rugged trails used by mahogany cutters through the Mountain Pine Ridge area. Apart from using rain water collected in old drums, the water source was a village well of brackish water. This well water used for all purposes was one of the worst kinds and definitely bad to drink. Cost of living there was the highest in my experience throughout the Colony.

The teacher's quarters where we stayed was inferior to many of the houses in the village. It consisted of the main house and a smaller kitchen hut, both built mostly of local forest material. The roof was thatched with long stem cohune leaves with forest twine used to tie them to wooden rafters. The walls of the main house were made of mud plastered on round sticks closely tied uprightly together but the walls of the kitchen hut were left unplastered to allow for in or out view. The pit latrine was also constructed with the same forest materials. This living arrangement after over forty years of teaching took me back almost full circle to those days when I had just begun teaching in San Antonio Toledo.

Here I labored for all these past months, feeling often broken and often very disappointed. Still I continued to give my best to the students and the community. With the school of about 85 children at the time, I had no problem with school attendance. Our relations with parents were satisfactory. Luckily for us, they spoke Spanish and a type of Maya (Yucatec) to which my family and I were somewhat familiar. The village leader, the alcalde, who was an elderly man showed much willingness to assist us as we settled in and to encourage the cooperation of the parents.

Toward the end of the first year, however, I developed a serious and persistent cough which, in spite of various local remedies continued unabated. The difficulty of commuting to El Cayo to get medical attention made it necessary for me to proceed to the Belize City Hospital. Here I was admitted and stayed for a month and a week, while my daughter Olivia acted as Principal. My son Constantine who was also teaching there assisted Olivia in managing the school. During this time it proved necessary for me to undergo a surgery to remove one of my lungs. This proved successful. I regained my health and returned to El Cayo where Constantine met me and we both proceeded to San Antonio on horses.

I resumed my duties very well and all was well until late the following year when I became so ill again that I decided it was time to retire with whatever little we had. Our family decided that we should all return home to Punta Gorda when school closed for Christmas vacation in December 1950. However, I could not continue the journey and had to be hospitalized here again in Belize City.

Now at my age, according to the Medical Department, my teaching days are over, and rightly so, because I should have given up long ago. But a teacher, even when weak from old age, had to force himself to continue his profession because there was no hope for a pension after retiring. Furthermore, with all the losses that my family suffered, I had to continue.

Hopefully when people of sympathy read the things I've told above, they would not refuse to assist me to be granted even a suitable compensation for all I have done for the Colony. In all forty-two years and two months; not counting those years I served as a pupil teacher.

# A Summary of the Teaching Service of Andres Enriquez

| | |
|---|---|
| 1901—1906 | Pupil teacher at the Punta Gorda School serving under Mr. Secundino Ogaldez, his former teacher and Head Teacher of same school from 1904-1908. Rev. Aloysius Averbeck, S.J. was also his teacher. |
| 1907—1917 | Re-opened the school at San Antonio Village, Toledo District and was stationed there as head teacher for ten years. |
| May 29, 1912 | Married Jane V. Villafranco who accompanied him to San Antonio and all other teaching posts. |
| 1917 | Head teacher at Forest Home School, Toledo District |
| 1918 | Head Teacher at Barranco Village, Toledo District |
| Sept. 5, 1918 | After the loss of five children due to miscarriage or at childbirth over the past few years, the first living child, Olivia Justiniana Enriquez was born in Punta Gorda |
| Feb. — April 1919 | Head teacher, Forest Home Village |
| June 1919 — April 1921 | Head teacher at El Cayo R.C. School |
| April 26, 1921 | Zenobia Celestina Enriquez born in El Cayo |
| June 1921— April 1929 | Head teacher at Progresso Village, Corozal District (Elicia, Solomon and Peter Enriquez were born here.) |
| June 1929— April 1930 | Barranco Village |
| Aug. 11, 1929 | Birth of Equitius Enriquez in Barranco |
| Aug, 1930 — Dec. 1931 | Teacher at TOPCO Estate. Toledo District. (Equitius died at TOPCO.) |
| Dec. 7, 1931 | Constantine Enriquez born in Punta Gorda. |
| Jan.—April 1932 | Head teacher at Crique Sarco Village, Toledo District. |
| June 1932— Feb.1949 | Head teacher at San Antonio Village, Toledo District The mission suddenly terminated his service. Protest made to the Education Office. |

| | |
|---|---|
| June 1949—<br>Dec. 1950 | The mission rescinded Andres Enriquez's termination and reinstalled him as Head teacher at San Antonio Village, Cayo District, one of the most remote and harsh teaching posts, especially for his age. Having suffered severe losses from hurricane and fire that destroyed the family home, Mr. Enriquez became very disappointed and "heartbroken" at the way the mission transferred him after over four decades of dedicated service at tremendous sacrifice to himself and his family. |
| June 8, 1950 | ***British Honduras Gazette*** Extraordinary, announces the appointment of Mr. Andres Enriquez to be a Member of the Most Excellent Order of the British Empire for his outstanding service in education in the colony of British Honduras. |
| July 2, 1950 | Congratulatory letter from Punta Gorda Carib Teachers stationed at various schools published in the Belize Billboard. Signed by: P. A. Albert Avila, teacher at Bullet Tree Falls, Cayo; Charles Martinez, teacher at Carmelita, Cayo; and Francisco Martinez teacher at Cristo Rey, Cayo. |
| Dec. 1950 | Mr. Enriquez medically retired due to failing health. Hospitalized at Belize City Hospital. |
| Dec. 24, 1950 | Received from His Excellency the Governor, Sir Ronald Harvey on behalf of His Majesty King George VI, the insignia of M.B.E. (Member of the Order of the British Empire) at his sick bed at the Belize City Hospital. |
| Jan. 25, 1951 | Died in Belize City hospital after over 42 years of outstanding teaching service at Roman Catholic schools in various communities of British Honduras. |
| Jan. 31, 1951 | Requiem High Mass offered in the morning at the Holy Redeemer Cathedral at which all teachers were invited. In attendance were also: the Acting Director of Education, Mr. Eric Brown, B.A. and Miss Kathleen Frazer, Secretary of the British Honduras Federation of Teachers. (***Belize Billboard***, Jan. 31, 1951) |

## Carib Teachers Proud Over Brother Theacer's M.B.E.

Editor, Sir:

We, the undersigned Carib teachers, would like the general public to know, particularly through the medium of the *Belize Billboard* that we are indeed gratefuly elated over the elevation of our hardworking and veteran schoolmaster Mr. Andres P Enriquez to the rank of Member of the Order of the British Empire, by His Majesty the King.

We also extend our most hearty congratulations to His Excellency Governor Sir Ronald Garvey for the knighthood bestowed upon him.

Lives of great men all remind us
We can make our lives sublime;
And departing leave behind us
Footprints in the sands of time,

        Yours, etc.

    P.A. Albert Avila
    Bullet Tree Fal's, Cayo

    Charles Martinez
    Carmelita, Cayo

    Francisco Martinez
    Cristo Rey, Cayo

*The Belize Billboard*, July 2, 1950

2798 SUPPLEMENT TO THE LONDON GAZETTE, 8 JUNE, 1950

Andres Patricio ENRIQUES, Esq., Headmaster, San Antonio, Cayo, British Honduras.
Michael Agbemezia EQUAGOO, Esq., Principal Officer of Customs and Excise Department, Nigeria.
Miss Kate Dorothy FERGUSON, Librarian, Regional Office of the British Council, Singapore.
Richard Campbell FORSTER, Esq., Chief Sanitary Inspector, City of Nairobi, Kenya.
Goh Chiang CHUAH, Office Assistant, Customs and Excise Department, Singapore.
Homeros Theodoulou HAJIDIMITRIOU, Esq, For public services in Cyprus.
Philip Seymour HAMMOND, Esq., Colonial Agricultural Service, Agricultural Officer, Gold Coast.
James Myers HANSEN, Esq., Office Assistant and Accountant, Police Force, Gold Coast.
William Thomas HARRINGTON, Esq., Chief Draughtsman, Survey Department, Nigeria.
George Charles Day HODGSON, Esq., Colonial Administrative Service, Secretary, African Foodstuffs Commission, Nyasaland.
Margaret Agnes, Mrs. CARR-HOLE, Clerk, Grade A, Agricultural Department, Kenya.
William Edwards HOLLANDS, Esq., Land

Alice Bhagwandai, Mrs. SINGH. For social and welfare services in British Guiana.
James Henry Evans SMART, Esq., Committee Clerk, Nairobi City Council, Kenya.
George Samuel SMITH, Esq., Chief Inspector of Stamps, Crown Agents for the Colonies.
Pierre Hubert SOODEEN, Esq., Establishment Assistant, Secretariat, Tanganyika.
Coralie Eugenie, Mrs. ST. AUBYN, Private Secretary to the Governor of Jamaica.
James STEVENSON, Esq., Land Officer and Senior Surveyor, Sierra Leone.
Charles William George STUART, Esq. For public services in Northern Rhodesia.
Sedelis TEMBAKAU, Esq., Deputy Assistant District Officer, North Borneo.
Constant Ernest TUBOKU-METZGER, Esq., Education Officer, Sierra Leone.
Balchandra Nanbhoy UPADHYIE, Accountant, Kamaran Sub-Treasury and Secretary, Kamaran Quarantine Station, Aden.
Datu Abang Yan bin Haji USOP, Senior Native Officer, Third Division, Sarawak.
Maria Francesca VANDEBEECK (Mother Mary Theodora), Head Mistress of Convent Primary School, Montserrat, Leeward Islands.

Announcement of New Members of the British Empire in the London Gazette 8 June 1950

THE BELIIZE BILLBOARD

## MBE Says "Thanks"

Mr. A. P. Enriquez, M. B. E., through the medium of this paper expresses his deep appreciation of the expressions of congratulations continued in the many letters and telegrams and verbal he received on the occasion of his appointment to the honour of being a Member of the Order of the British Empire conferred on him lately, and begs all concerned to help with their prayers that he may live up to the standard required by such honour.

He also apologises for the lateness of this announcement, due to the influx of those correspondences over an extended period.

The Belize Billboard, July 13th, 1950

## Teacher M.B.E. In P.G.

Mr A. P. Enriquez, M.B.E. and Mrs. Enriquez arrived in Punta Gorda recently to take up permanent residence in their hometown.

Mr. Enriquez who retired after 42 years of teaching in various B.H. villages is suffering from a lung ailment.

Mr Enriqeuz was recently awarded the M.B.E. in recognition of his service to B. H. educations.

*The Belize Billboard*, January 22nd, 1951

## Teacher M.B.E. Dies

*The Belize Billboard*, Jan. 26, 1951

FORMER schoolmaster Andres Enriquez, M.B.E, died at Punta Gorda last night.

After 42 years of school teaching, Mr. Enriquez retired at the end of 1950 on account of ill-health.

He received his insignia of M.B.E. in a private ceremony at the Belize Hospital Christmas Eve 1950.

A Requiem High mass will be offered on Wednesday, January 31, at 5:30 p.m. in the Holy Redeemer Cathedral. All teachers are especially invited to attend.

## Nuguya, Jane Victoriana Enriquez nee Villafranco*

It is with great pleasure that I write this, my experiences during 38 years of married life and of traveling with my husband, Andres Patricio Enriquez, who taught all over the colony of British Honduras.

I was born in Punta Gorda, Toledo District, on the 12th day of July in the year 1895. My deceased father, Louis Majin Villafranco, was a native of Spanish Honduras. My mother, Antonia Villafranco nee Zuniga, was born in Punta Gorda on September 3, 1871. Her parents were Martin Zuniga and Petrona Felice Labriel. My mother is now 78 years old, and is yet able to do all her housework.

I also have four younger sisters: Gertrude also known as Nitu Bibi, Faustina Kate also known as Nitu Keta, Barbara also called Nitu Tu, and Pastora. The only surviving brother I have is Joseph Claro Villafranco, the sixth and last child of my parents. Our elder brother, Desiderius Villafranco, who was the fifth child died when he was only two months old.

My parents consented to my marriage to Mr. Andres Enriquez, a teacher now deceased. The wedding took place at the St. Peter Claver Church in Punta Gorda on the 29th day of May in the year 1912 when I was 16 years old. Mr. Enriquez who was born on November 12, 1886, was 25 years old at the time of our marriage.

After becoming married, I began my life of traveling with my husband and gained many experiences through living among other races of people quite different from our own. Since I became married, I did not think it right to stay away from my husband for long periods of time. I traveled with him wherever he went.

---

* "*Nuguya*" means "I" when spoken by the Garifuna female.

Jane V. Enriquez, 1895 – 1968

Antonia Villafranco (1871-1957), mother of Jane Enriquez nee Villafranco

The day of our departure to San Antonio came one day in early June, about one week after we had gotten married. That morning our neighbours and relatives all gathered at my parents' home to bid us farewell.

This was both a happy and sad time for my family. They were happy that in this first time that I was leaving home, I was in the hands of a highly respected teacher — Mr. Enriquez. The sadness that they felt was because I was going to live far away in the wilderness where no other member of my family had ever been. We would never know what situations we would meet. Furthermore, for months at a time until the school vacation, they would not see or hear from us.

Some of the relatives advised me as best they could about how to be a good wife. They reminded me to always be prayerful especially when I met with hardships during my travels. They all wished me good luck.

My mother, having already given so much advice when she had consented to my marriage, did not say much that day. All she said to Mr. Enriquez in our native Garifuna language was, "You now have my first daughter; she is going with you and will be with you for the rest of your life. If ever she disobeys you or misbehaves, please let me know."

While our visitors were mingling and chatting, my husband made his final check of our luggage to make sure that we had all we needed, and that our load was not too heavy to carry on the long trek. Soon after, he announced that it was time to depart. Everyone embraced me as they said their goodbyes. It was sad to see my sisters and little brother crying as I embraced them. My mother hid herself in the bedroom so as not to see me depart.

Later that afternoon, my husband and I departed Punta Gorda to start our long journey to San Antonio Village in the Toledo District to reopen the new school year. That was the beginning of our long journey of life together. Sadly, my little sisters followed me to a far distance crying. They did not want me to leave. Quite often I turned around to tell them to go home; instead they cried even more. For a few moments, I even had second thoughts about returning with them for it was not easy to leave my parents' home. My husband and I continued anyway, and my sisters eventually returned home.

I knew from the stories he had shared with me before we had gotten married that walking the entire journey of a little over twenty-five miles would be rough and would take about two days. That didn't matter; I was glad to be with him.

The first night we slept at Rancho, an American settlement that was also known as the Toledo Settlement. There at the family home of one of my husband's friends, we were kindly treated. Early the following day we started the rest of the journey. This was a very hard, long and tiring walk on a trail through the forest. For the whole journey, my husband carried on his back, a load of bags that contained such items as a few pieces of clothing and beddings while I carried the basket of food.

As we walked I remembered the stories he had shared about his experiences on this trail. Along the way he pointed out places he had told me about. I laughed when he showed me the place where he had tripped, fallen and gotten all muddy the year before. It was always funny the way he shared the story.

I shuddered when he showed me the swamps where many horses became stuck and had to be left there to slowly die while vultures circled overhead. We had to wade through that swamp step by step with the help of our staff, often with mud up to our thighs. I became frightened when he showed me a huge snake crossing the path just ahead of us near one of the old woodcutters' camps. Each time I became afraid, he reminded me that everything was going to be alright. I felt safe following behind him. He knew every part of the trail very well. It was the first time then that I saw what he had been experiencing over the past five years that he had been traveling to reach the village.

As we drew nearer to San Antonio, we crossed the Murphy Die Creek. Within two miles of our destination, the level trails and terrain gave way to a succession of hills. From the top of one of the hills that we were crossing, my husband showed me the church standing at a distance on top of another high hill in the village. The view through the fog made it seem as though the church was floating on the surface of a lake or as if it was in the middle of a savannah. It was such a wonderful sight. The church went out of sight as we descended the hill but another view of the village was seen from about half mile as we approached. This time we saw that a big cross stood in front of the church and the church compound which included the school and teacher's quarters, was fenced in with sapodilla sticks.

After this view we had coming down from the last hill, we saw nothing else of the village as we walked through the forest trails until at last we reached the village gate. In those days, the whole village was fenced with sapodilla sticks and growing trees. I was told that the village fence was the only way to keep the hogs from going into the plantations. As soon as we entered the gate, we waded into a little creek where we washed off the mud from our legs and feet. From the creek at the village entrance we walked up, up and up the hill until we arrived at our new home at about four o'clock that evening, very tired and worn out.

San Antonio in the 1940s

## San Antonio

Early the next morning, I stepped outside our thatched teachers' house on top of the central hill near the school and gazed at the green forested natural hills and valleys that surrounded the village. Mr. Enriquez explained that there were ancient Maya mounds here and there in the area. The scenery and the surroundings looked so beautiful. The village looked circular in shape. On top of the hills and in the valleys I saw small patches of brown thatched roofs of the traditional homes. There were also plantation plots scattered around in the distance. For a long moment, I admired the beauty

(*above*) Bishop Murphy visiting San Antonio in 1931.
Jane Enriquez is the Garifuna woman to the left of the center behind the children.

(*below*) Maya girls and women in the 1930s

and quiet of this new scenery. It was the first time that I was seeing such a place. That morning and for many days after, when I gazed at the hills, I felt the same sense of peace as I got when I stood at the seashore in Punta Gorda to gaze across the wide calm sea.

Our house was built of thatched roof and had an earthen floor just like the homes in the village. There were two houses—the main house where we slept and ate and the smaller kitchen hut next door where I did the cooking on the fire hearth. Our bed was a rough wooden frame made of four low posts that were driven to the ground and connected with cross sticks. Across these sticks the bark of the Moho tree is stretched and tied. There was no mattress. We used mats that were woven from another dried plant. Sometimes when I was alone at home during the day, I rested in the hammock.

I found the villagers to be very welcoming and friendly although I did not understand a single word of their language. Whenever any of the native women came to our quarters they brought along some corn tortillas and a calabash with a sort of drink made of ground cacao mixed with tortilla and black pepper. After receiving these with a friendly smile, I only said "Gracias," for I did not know a word in their language. Whenever they spoke, my husband interpreted for me. Since he had been living there years before, he was already at home in their culture and spoke their language thoroughly.

The following Sunday after our arrival at San Antonio, my husband took me for a long walk around the village to visit and get to know the people. Before we left our house, he explained that whenever the people offered anything I must not refuse it or show any sign of dislike otherwise they would be offended and never again offer us anything. At every house we visited, the usual greeting was "Dios." That was the first word I learned in the language. There was no difference between good morning, good evening, or good night; all was the same "Dios." After the usual greetings they offered us a seat and something to eat or drink. At some houses, we were seated on wooden boxes; at others we sat on blocks of wood about six inches high; and yet at others, we sat in string hammocks made of henequen strings. I admired how my husband spoke with them so fluently in their own Maya language.

As I was introduced to the families, I learnt new Maya surnames such as Ico, Cal, Buul, Bolon, Assi, Chiac, Pop, Cho, Rash, Chi, Sho, and Ixim. What struck me was that these names stood out quite differently than Garifuna surnames like Castillo, Palacio, Arana, Lopez and Zuniga, which are really Spanish surnames that were given to our people. The sounds of the different Maya surnames were interesting for me to hear that day and when I mentioned this to my husband all he said was, "You'll soon get used to them."

That Sunday evening shortly after our home visits, my brother-in-law, Sylverius Enriquez, the younger and only brother of my husband, arrived in San Antonio to give me the sad news of the sudden death of my dear father. That was my first sad experience. For this to happen so soon after my marriage and only one week after I had left home to that faraway place felt too much for me. We were very grateful, however, that my brother-in-law walked all the way from Punta Gorda to give me this news or I would not have known until we returned home in December. My husband and I then decided that it was best for me to return home for a short time to be with my mother and sisters.

Immediately the following morning, about one week after I had arrived, I walked the same long trail back to Punta Gorda with my brother-in-law. I could not be there in time for the funeral but I was glad to be with my mother, sisters and little brother around that time. I stayed at home with them for a month.

In the month of July, I returned to San Antonio to settle properly with my husband and to make myself at home.

The first thing I did soon after I settled in was to make friends with the people and to learn my way around the village. Everywhere I went I saw the women stealing glances or staring at me with a sort of puzzled look. As soon as I stared back they shifted their eyes to the ground or elsewhere. I realized that for almost all of them it was the first time that they were seeing a Garifuna woman. They seemed to watch my every move. It was also strange for them seeing a woman who was much taller than them. Gradually they got used to me and became very friendly.

Although most of the adults could not speak English, some of them spoke a little Spanish besides their native Maya language. That made it a bit easier for me to talk with them. Luckily, as a young child I had learned to speak some Spanish from my father who, as I mentioned before, was from Honduras. The little bit of Spanish that the Mayas spoke helped me during those early days to talk with them. At first I asked them to tell me in Maya, the names of different things and they were so kind as to teach me. They in turn asked me for the English names of the same things and I taught them. At home I practiced the new words with my husband and he corrected my mistakes. Gradually I learned more and more of the native language.

That first week while my husband worked at school, I went around with the Maya women to learn where to fetch water for cooking and drinking, and where to wash clothes. In order to fetch water for cooking, I followed the women all the way down a hill to a well that was dug by their ancestors who had been the first to settle in the village. That well was not as deep as the Punta Gorda wells where we had to use a long rope tied to a bucket to draw out water.

At the village well, I noticed a common practice in which the women first fetched water to wash their feet, faces and arms, before filling the jugs. When the well was full, they dipped water with their buckets or jugs and when it was low they used a calabash to fill their receptacles. In those days the villagers mostly used jugs that they made out of clay. After they filled their jugs, they carried two at a time—one on their head which they held with one hand, and the other along their side, which they held with the other hand. Soon I learned that the well was used to get water for drinking and cooking only.

After filling our buckets, we all had to walk uphill to reach our homes. At first, every time I returned home with my bucket of water, I had to sit on the ground two or three times along the way to take a rest because I panted so hard that I felt as though my heart would burst out of my inside. Before long, however, I could run up and down the hills as easily as the natives.

All washing and bathing were done at the river. It was a great inconvenience to do these at home since it was too far to fetch water only for these purposes. To get to the river I had to walk down another hill with some of the women. There they taught me how to wash clothes in their native way. They all stood knee deep in the river while they rubbed each soaked piece of clothing on the flat river stones that they placed along the river bank.

At times in between the silence of their washing, some of the women shared their personal stories or news about what was happening in the village. Walking uphill with the load of washed clothes was another experience I had to get used to. At first, I imitated their way of washing but I did not like the idea of standing in the water for so long. A few months later I brought along my own washbasin from home in Punta Gorda to wash at the bank of the river instead of standing in the water.

During those early days, I also found it very difficult to get accustomed to the different kinds of Maya food, as it was altogether different from my native Garifuna food. It was from our neighbours and friends that I first learned to eat many of the local foods. Gradually I learned to eat whatever they ate. They always served their food in calabashes called luts, and ate using their fingers.

Corn tortilla was always part of their main dish but they also ate various herbs, shoots, fruits and ground food. After much practice, I also learned to grind corn and bake corn tortillas. The grinding was not done with the new hand-crank corn mill as we are doing now. All the grinding was done on a flat rubbing stone called *metate*. After the corn was boiled in lime water until it became soft,

Maya woman baking tortillas, 1911. On her table is the *lek*, in which tortillas are stored.

it was washed thoroughly and placed on the metate. With another long round stone the women rubbed the soft corn over and over until it became a fine dough. They then took a piece of the dough, shaped it into a small ball, placed it on a piece of banana leaf and flattened it with their fingers until it is round. Then they placed the flat round dough to bake on the *comal*, a flat round iron sheet, that was heated over the fire hearth. As soon as each tortilla was baked, it was wrapped in a cloth inside a large round calabash container, called *lek*, to keep hot.

I learned to use the metate quickly enough but when it came time for baking the tortillas, I found it very difficult. It took me several weeks before I learned to make tortillas as well as the natives. The tortillas I first made were badly shaped; they were too long or too square, far from perfectly round as those made by the women and often too dry. The women teased me and laughed at the result. At the same time, they were always patient and kind. After long and constant practice I became perfect at it. Apart from teaching me to make tortillas, the women painstakingly taught me their way of life and I always thank them very much for that.

I also learned to prepare the cacao drink; this was far easier than making tortillas. First the cacao beans, called *kuku*, are taken out from the pod, placed out in the sun for a few days to dry, and then roasted over the fire hearth on the comal. After roasting the beans are ground on the metate in the same way that corn is ground. The ground cacao is then mixed with corn flour that is made from roasted ground corn tortillas, and then soaked in water before grinding again on the metate. That mixture is then placed on the fire hearth and boiled with some black pepper added as a spice.

Different kinds of corn or cacao drinks were usually served with meals or in between meals. One of the most popular drinks is called *posol*. This is a thick porridge that is made by grinding the soft boiled corn used for making tortillas and mixing it with hot or cold water. Another common drink is called *pinol*, which they make from ground roasted grains of corn mixed with hot water and sugar.

Whenever I returned home from visiting families and learning my way around the village, I told my husband about all that I saw and what the people gave me. One day he mentioned that he noticed I was eating some foods that he himself had not eaten before. He warned me to be careful about eating too many varieties of new foods or too much of the new food all at once as these could be harmful to my health. It will take time for my body to get accustomed to this change of foods, he explained.

Soon the people spread the news around the village that I had learned to prepare and eat their kind of food.

It seemed like such big news because in many of my conversations with the women they said, "I heard that you now know how to make corn tortillas," or "Your neighbor told me that you like posol," or whatever they heard that I had made or eaten.

In those days, the Mayas very rarely used lard, used little or no sugar, and did not really eat much meat. Occasionally a pig was killed; the lard from it was preserved in pint bottles, and was used sparingly with crushed pepper. Most often, when anybody killed a pig, the meat would never be eaten even though they sold it as cheaply as five cents a pound. What surprised me was the fact that they gathered all the chicarones in a leaf, tied it in a bundle and just stored it.

Sometimes they mixed dried pepper into a paste by adding salt and a little water. This they ate with hot corn tortillas. For many of them, this seemed to serve as a grand dinner. At other times, they had green crushed pepper and salt for dinner. The use of black beans was also common and this was much preferred over red beans. The planting of red beans was mostly for sale in Punta Gorda or sent by boat to be sold in Belize.

The greens or herbs that I learned to eat were usually boiled and seasoned with crushed pepper and salt. These included the *kulá*, a purple leaf herb whose tender shoots are collected young and boiled or fried with the usual seasonings. They also ate *tzuk*, the young shoot of a particular palm eaten with salt and pepper. Then there was *kuúl*, the tender part of the cohune palm also known as cohune cabbage, eaten raw or boiled. Another native food was *mabuy*, the ripe berry of an orange color herb, boiled, strained and mixed with *tzuk, kulá, kuúl*, or a combination. The fresh shoot of the coco-yam plant is also boiled then fried and eaten with tortillas. The corn porridge is made unsweetened because sugar could not be found anywhere. The annato, also known as the *kutzub*, is another plant that grows all around the village. The people used this for making a red food seasoning.

Occasionally, the young men went out in the evenings to trap wild animals such as ground-mole, spider monkeys, howler monkeys, gibnut, agouti or armadillo or birds, such as parrots, wild turkeys and chachalaca. Some men used a blowgun to catch these animals. For meat the Mayas also ate jotes, also called *tutú*, which are fresh water snails. Jotes is usually seasoned with cowfoot leaf and pepper.

Most of the time, though, there was hardly any meat to eat and whenever I complained they said, "We are tired of eating or seeing meat."

"But there is no meat," I said.

"Oh! Indeed we are very tired of beans or pepper." But they said this only to repeat my complaint, as if to make fun of what I was saying; they did not seem to mind it at all.

We also found plenty of other types of food in the village — yam, yampee, sweet potato, coco, cassava root, banana, plantain — all of which I did not use to find enjoyable to prepare without meat. Whenever I went in search of chicken or meat, the people showed me the very small ones of about three or four weeks old. I walked from house to house in search of eggs or beans or anything to buy but the natives either did not have any or were more inclined to keep them for their own diet. Many times I became puzzled and wondered what to cook. Sometimes I even felt like throwing away the money I had in my hand. We had nothing else to eat but to go back to the native meal, which is pepper and salt. When we had lard, I added only a little to the mixture since it was so scarce and hard to get.

Over the next few months I gradually gathered all my local kitchen utensils such as a long flat thick board on which to keep my metate, a few earthen jars and pots, and a comal for baking tortillas. Everything pertaining to the kitchen at that time was earthenware made by the native women. However, cooking in these pots took so long that after some time, I replaced them with metal utensils that I brought from home in Punta Gorda. Pretty soon, I had begun to understand more words in Maya so that whenever I met any villager I could explain myself fairly well.

During my first few months in the village, I noticed that as a stranger, I had to be very careful when I visited some of the homes.

Boat travel by teachers to various teaching posts at various Toledo villages in the early 1900s would resemble this scene of boats resting after miles of paddle along the coast, upstream through creeks and rivers, to reach their destination.

As soon as the dogs heard the sound of my footsteps on the stones, they would bark and run. What was more surprising was that the children screamed when they saw me since they had never seen a coloured woman before. Whenever I visited a home, I approached slowly and gently. Before reaching the door I made a sound with either my feet or throat to alert the family of my approach. Mr. Enriquez had warned me that if a visitor suddenly showed up at their door, they would get very frightened and sickness would follow. This sickness, locally known as *hakul-olil*, comes as a result of a sudden fright.

If someone became ill with fright, one of the elders would go and ask the one who caused the fright for some of his or her hair or a piece of his or her garment to burn under the patient who would be lying in a hammock. The villagers believed that if they did not get any of these things, the frightened one would get so seriously sick as to vomit worms. In such cases, their bush doctor would be called to examine the patient. The cases would often be diagnosed as "the living spirit." The pulse would beat fast and the stomach would be much hardened and swollen. Then the bush doctor would give his patient proper attention. If the patient had a fever, the bush doctor would say, "he is very seriously ill and no one knows whether he will recover from this sickness." Therefore, as strangers to the village, we had to be very careful when approaching the people at first until they got used to us.

I also noticed that whenever any visitor came to our dwelling, my husband took great pains to speak to them in a soft low voice (for they never spoke loud) and listen to them in the way that a fond father listens to his children. He was like a father to them, listening patiently to their big and small matters. I was quick to imitate the way my husband interacted with them. Because he was living among them five years before I arrived, I was certain that he knew them better than me.

## *Christmas Vacation*

In the month of December, I was a few months pregnant, so we had to decide whether to remain in San Antonio for the Christmas holidays or return home to Punta Gorda. To travel home would have been very difficult. Because of the rainy season, the trail from San Antonio to Punta Gorda always put on what we call "full suit." We decided it was best to spend the holidays with our family.

We finally arranged with some Maya guides to travel with us to Punta Gorda through another route that passed through Conejo, a little settlement of a few Q'eq'chi families at that time. From Conejo we took a dory to Punta Gorda. This route was taken in order to avoid the heavy strain of walking the twenty-five-mile-long muddy trail especially in my pregnant condition. We spent that night at Conejo.

Early the following day, we started our journey from a different and strange place. We took a long walk through a wild muddy path, not exactly sure where it would lead us. Somehow, however, we got to a landing at around one o'clock that afternoon. We spent about half an hour loading the dory that the men hired for us and then continued our journey by river.

We did not travel far that afternoon when we decided that it was best to set up camp near the riverbanks before the night set in. The Maya guides and Mr. Enriquez unloaded the dory. While I prepared dinner from the food we packed, they gathered materials from the forest to build a temporary shelter for the night. The camp was made by tying the ends of four sticks to a crosspiece with tie-ties, then laying some cohune leaves on top. The bed for my husband and I were made of cohune leaves that were placed on the

Map of southern Belize showing villages that existed in 1910. Dotted lines indicate trails.

ground inside. The Maya strung their hammocks under some trees where they slept in the open forest.

Later that evening as the sun was setting, we heard the strange cry of a wild bird. One of the men looking very frightened said in Spanish, "*Alla va el diablo!*" or there goes the devil.

Since I had never slept in the jungle before that night, I had believed what the man said and became so frightened that I said to myself, "This surely is the night for wild beasts to devour me and I will not see my mother again."

The night was so dark that I could not see anything. I was so afraid that I hardly slept. Besides the sound of the flowing river, I could hear every sound in the forest all through the night. Very soon after I managed to fall asleep, dawn broke and it was time to prepare for a long day of travel. I woke up feeling very tired.

Early that morning, we continued our river journey in the dory. At that time there was no one settling along the river. Neither was there anything to see along the river banks except the wild forest. We traveled all day down the river and then by sea until we reached Punta Gorda that evening.

All our friends and relatives were glad to see us arrive home in good health. We spent a very happy Christmas holiday with the rest of our family.

## *Return to San Antonio*

Early the following year, 1913, we returned to San Antonio through the trail that would later become the Punta Gorda—San Antonio road, and reached our destination the next day. The villagers were glad to see us return to them. They brought us some tortillas and unsweetened cacao drink. By this time, I had begun to get accustomed to their native food. We arrived very tired and hungry and were so glad for the food that the people offered us.

Apart from Mr. Enriquez and me, there was no other race of people living in the village with the natives. Once in a while the Hindus from Rancho came to buy hogs. The Roman Catholic priest visited San Antonio every three or four months but stayed only for a week or so.

It was mostly during the school hours, when my husband was at school and I was alone at home, that I would take a break from my household duties to visit my neighbours.

As time went on, I made myself more at home in the village. I made more friends with the villagers, learned more of the Maya language as well as their customs. I saw how they made their earthen pots, earthen comals, earthen basins, and all their kitchen utensils. It was they who taught me to sew the cross-stitch style and sew the designs that they make on their blouses.

One day I went to one of the neighbour's home and found her sewing a skirt and blouse for herself in preparation for an upcoming fiesta. The woman told me to try the clothing on, and when I did, the mother, sister-in-law, children and everyone in the house came around me saying how well the dress fitted me. They said that they must sew one like it for me.

I went home with the dress on, to show my husband and to tell him about the fiesta. However, I did not finish explaining when he scolded, "Oh nonsense! Go and take off those old things. I did not bring you here for that."

At the fiestas I noticed that the people perform many types of dances—Devil Dance, Monkey Dance, Moro and Cortez Dance.

The Deer Dance was always done in honor of San Luis, the patron saint of San Antonio.

Around that time, there were no horses in or around San Antonio. Because the road was very muddy and the distance was too far to Punta Gorda, it seemed too cruel to send for additional items with those people who occasionally went to town. We had to make do with whatever we found in the village and we gradually became accustomed to this. Since I had begun to speak the language and understand more of it, I never felt any loneliness even though my mother, four sisters and little brother were far way at home in Punta Gorda.

When I went out to buy anything, I tried hard to speak mostly in the native language. Perhaps some of the words were badly pronounced and others were well said but I just kept on without being ashamed of learning. At first, some of the people did not seem to understand what I was saying and therefore they did not know what I wanted. Others guessed more or less what I meant to say and corrected me. Some only laughed. Such was the case until I learned to master their language well.

Most of the children in the village suffered from symptoms of malnutrition. They looked pale and felt very light in weight for their age. Some were bloated and puffy. All this was due to the poor diet of their mothers, especially during pregnancy, and the poor nourishment their mothers gave their children. Their firstborns were very tender and looked like premature babies not being at all lively at birth or early childhood. Remember that the mothers were usually only twelve to thirteen years old. Because they got married at such a young age, they looked weary and lacked the energy to take such great responsibilities of parenthood. It was also common to see children three to four years old still being breastfed.

The children also started to work hard at a very young age. Usually by the time they were seven years old they were already carrying loads of corn, firewood and other things from the milpa to their home. They took these loads in a crocus bag on their back with the weight supported by a piece of bark, called "*mecapal*", across their forehead. At their homes these children were also in charge of feeding the pigs and chickens.

Even though Mr. Enriquez insisted that the children attend school every day, there were times when parents took them out of school for a few days to work in the milpa. Sometimes the parents also made the older children stay at home to take care of the younger ones while the parents went to the milpa. There were times when Mr. Enriquez found it necessary to strongly warn the parents to discourage this practice that happens especially during the planting and harvest season.

It was at San Antonio that for the first time I saw boys and girls getting married. The boys marry at the age of sixteen and the girls at the age of twelve or thirteen. Just before, or as soon as their children become a teenager, many parents took their children out of school and arranged for them to get married.

Marriage is usually arranged by the parents of the boy. It is they who select the girl for their son and make an agreement with her parents for their son to marry her. When they became engaged, the boy's parents offered the girl's parents gifts such as pigs. Within a short period of time they arranged the marriage and the priest conducted the ceremony in the church during one of his visits. For the marriage ceremony the boys put on such tremendously big pants just to look big and tall while the girls wore such long skirts. The young man was responsible for all expenses for the marriage celebration. He had to buy the wedding dress and pay for food and drinks for the celebration. A few months after the wedding he also had to get a house built, and provide all the necessary furnishing. Usually the parents assisted their son to get this done.

I noticed that many young fathers in their teenage years worked very hard to take care of their families. I believe that they were too young for such responsibilities. They had to carry tremendous loads of corn, beans or firewood from the milpa such that anyone could see that they could hardly walk up and down the hills. Usually they bore their load quietly without admitting pain. Because of all the strain of regularly carrying heavy loads and forcing their nature to mature before its time, some of the young men soon got very sick and bloated, and died at a very young age by the time they had two or three children.

One very bad habit the people had was bathing in the cold river when their bodies were still hot immediately after being near the fire hearth or working in the plantations under the blazing sun. The boys and men, after carrying a heavy load or working hard in the heat of the broiling sun just went to the cold river to bathe. As a result, many suffered from a sallow complexion, fever, then pains in their joints, feelings of tiredness, enlarged spleen, and hardened liver, until they finally died.

Usually life was very peaceful in San Antonio. However, the drunkenness that always happened during festivities was one of the biggest problems. During these festivities several of the men would drink rum that they bought from Punta Gorda. They also drank locally made alcoholic drinks such as *baluch*, a drink made from fermented honey and the bark of the *balche* tree and *chicha*, a wine made from fermented corn and sugar cane. When the men got drunk, they were usually very rowdy. Very often as they staggered around the village they could be seen with blood flowing from their wounded head, nose, lips, face and arms. Once in a while a few of the women also got drunk.

When they were not drunk the men were usually friendly, mannerly and good-natured. But when they became drunk they often talked and cried about past problems or conflicts that they seemed to have kept quietly to themselves in their sober state. Others went back to personal quarrels they had with another months before and this usually resulted in fights using fists or rocks. Sometimes these drunken fights led to serious injuries, chopping wounds or even murder. Over the years that I have been in San Antonio every violent fight or murder that happened (although very few) was done by drunken men. Some of the most serious arguments that led to murder usually had to do with jealousy over women. It was also common for drunken men to beat their wives at home, even after these wives struggled to carry them home.

The very disturbing behavior that results from the heavy drinking and drunkenness was often a big concern for Mr. Enriquez and the priests. Mr. Enriquez often discussed this problem with Fr. Tenk. During one of his visits to the village Fr. Tenk saw this behavior at a fiesta and at Mass strongly reminded the villagers about the dangers of their drinking. At village meetings or church service, Mr. Enriquez often tried his best to keep talking to the men about this behavior but the drunkenness at festivities was very difficult to control.

One of the things I admired about the people was their custom of working together and helping one another to build their houses, to clear their plantations or to harvest their crops. When there was a big task to get done, the people formed groups and provided labor for each other. For example, if a family wanted to build a house, a group of men would volunteer to build the house at no cost. When others wanted to have theirs built or to cut the plantation, the group would also assist. As the men provided labor, the women got together to cook the meals to feed the workers. Instead of using money that most of them didn't have, they helped one another with their labor. In that way they could own their house or start their own plantations.

The clothing that the Mayas wore was very simple. To me, the men's pants looked somewhat like pajamas. It looked as though the local tailor somehow tore the material, sewed it together and inserted an extra square piece in the crotch to make it convenient for walking. Both sides were slit and there were no pockets whatsoever on the pants—four strings were sewn together to tie at the waist. The shirts looked grand as though they were ready-made. No doubt these had been brought to the village from somewhere else. The shirts had a double bosom, collar, long sleeves and open cuffs, with all parts neatly sewn with backstitch.

All sewing was done by hand as no one could afford sewing machines at that time. The men also did not wear drawers or any sort of underwear. Shirts and pants were worn on their bare skin. Whenever they lifted up their shirts or when they were without shirts their naked hips and lower backs were seen. The shirts that they used were made long and left to hang loose over the pants. The boys wore long pants and kept their hair long and bushy. Gradually the people began to improve on the clothing by lining the front part of the pants and putting on two pockets. So whenever any fiesta occurred, they put on the better made clothing over the old-style ones. On special occasions the men also wore their rubber boots or tennis as a part of their dress.

The men's hair was always trimmed in the same style. A little peak was left at the back of the head. The trimming interval was very long and the hair was left to grow long until it reached their shoulders and eyebrows. Young and old men wore black felt hats.

The older women wore long skirts, usually of red print cloth, and each skirt was made of several yards of material. Two rows of frills and four rows of coloured braids were sewn on their skirts. Their blouses were made with white cotton cloth. Around the neck and sleeves were embroidered patterns of birds, flowers or other patterns that the women stitch by hand. These patterns were stitched with black threads onto strips of white cotton cloth that would then be sewn to the blouse.

Plenty of necklaces from stringed beads were usually worn around the neck and all wore the same pattern of earrings. Finger rings were of tin and silver. The hair was plaited with cotton braid and was tied with it at the end of the hair. For head covering, the women also wore square shawls or shawls with tassels on the edges. Their ancestors brought this same custom with them from San Luis, Guatemala. The girls sometimes wore a long blouse and always a single piece of clothing over their bare bodies.

The men and women often stayed half-naked at home. The younger children stayed fully naked. Quite often the older women walked about the community naked to the waist with their bare breasts exposed. It was surprising for me to see girls up to ten or eleven years old walking fully naked in the presence of everyone and anyone in the village. They would go the creek for a bath and return home naked. The older girls wore clothes like their mothers to cover the lower half of their bodies. The upper half was left bare with their breasts fully exposed.

Girls went to school in long blouses and the boys, like their fathers, wore the same clothing. The younger boys went in long shirts. The poorer girls and orphans refused to go to school because they had very little or no clothing.

So that the people did not use clothing as an excuse for not sending their children to school, Mr. Enriquez encouraged them to attend school with whatever they had as long as they were fully covered even if it meant using the same clothes over and over. In order to fully cover themselves, and since it was not usual for them to cover the top of their bodies, these girls wore the long skirts of an older sister or relative and pulled it all the way to their underarm and supported each side with strings tied from one part of the skirt around each shoulder.

Christmas season was approaching and, to make it special, Mr. Enriquez and I planned an entertainment for the school. The children practiced to perform short plays, to sing and dance. After a month's practice with the school children we began to get ready for the show. I sewed the girls' dresses and did my best with the girls while my husband did his part with the boys. The Rev. Fr. Tenk S.J. (may he rest in peace) was on his visit to the village at that time and

Garifuna women in Punta Gorda with a priest in 1915

so, on the night of the entertainment, he played the church organ at intervals. It was the first time that an entertainment had taken place at San Antonio, and oh, it was grand. There was a large crowd and the natives were pleased to observe the advancement of their children.

## *Traveling to and from Punta Gorda*

Then came the month of April when the school holidays began. We went down to Punta Gorda to spend the May vacation at home. I suffered very much on that journey and thought I would not reach Punta Gorda safely. Think of twenty-five miles for a pregnant woman to walk and yet arrive at her destination on the same day! When I got home my feet were very swollen and I was very tired.

Sadly, in the month of May that year, I gave birth to a stillborn baby boy. When school re-opened in June, I did not return to San Antonio but remained at home till the month of August.

A new school was opened at Aguacate in June 1913 and Mr. Santiago Labriel, a relative of mine and a close friend of my husband, was assigned to teach in that village.

In August 1913, Mr. Labriel traveled down from the village of Aguacate to Punta Gorda to get his family. Mr. Enriquez also came to take me back to San Antonio. Both Mr. Labriel and my husband met at our home and they decided to return to their posts by the farmer's route. That was on a Saturday.

By Sunday morning, we were all sailing down the coast from Punta Gorda. When we arrived at Moho River we were faced with the problems of high flood and strong river current. We had a very large dory with nine men who took turns to paddle. In the dory, there were also Mrs. Labriel, her little son William (who later went to work with the American Company at Puerto Barrios) and Dionicio Williams who was a schoolboy and later became a tailor. Altogether, there were fourteen of us. As soon as we entered near the mouth of the river, the strong current drifted us far out to sea. The men had to paddle much harder to gain entrance to the mouth of the river.

Interestingly the Mayas did not paddle like Garifuna people. Instead of working together when they paddled, each one paddled the way he feels like. Their way of paddling was often amusing and seeing this, the people from Punta Gorda can often tell from afar what group of people was approaching the coast. The Garifuna people in Punta Gorda had the habit of looking everywhere along the coast then across the wide sea for approaching or passing vessels. This was their way of finding out who was coming and what was happening with the outer world.

When they returned home they would be asked by family members, "Did you see anything new or strange when you were out? Did anybody new arrive today?"

Sometimes the answer was, "I saw some people coming in a dory and they look like Indians."

The dory that the Mayas used could be recognized from afar off at sea because of the way they paddled.

Anyway, because of the strong currents we did not travel far. When evening came we stopped at a Spanish settler's cottage along the river bank to rest for the night. Early the following day we started our journey again. This time, the river was more flooded and the current was stronger. We traveled all day and because of the flood and swamp, we could not find anywhere along the river bank to come out of the dory. We stopped only once to tie the dory to the bough of a tree to have lunch and rest. At around five o'clock that evening, after having traveled a good distance for the day, we stopped at the home of a Maya family to spend the night.

Early the next morning, Monday, the mistress of the house got up to rub some corn on the metate and baked tortillas. I also woke up early to help her. We all ate some hot tortillas for breakfast before starting our journey again.

We continued our journey very slowly against the strong river currents and over the falls. At times we all pulled our way upstream by holding on to bushes along the water's edge. Long at last we found a fairly dry spot along the riverbank nearer to the falls. We all came out of the dory and walked along the river while the men hauled the dory through the falls. By the way they managed the dories, the Maya men showed that they had a lot of knowledge and experience in traveling on the river especially under these conditions. Somehow we felt safe and were all very confident that even through those strong currents of the flooded river we would never capsize. That would have been deadly.

The farther we went up the river, the stronger the current became, such that we had to use ropes and poles more often than paddles. If by accident, the dory would turn cross-wise, it would surely capsize. Sometimes along the way, I even wondered why people came to live in this part of the country where there was so much difficulty to travel by water. Or why we even had to come this far, make all this sacrifice and risk our lives to serve them.

We continued on our journey until we safely and thankfully reached the Aguacate landing. After unloading for half an hour, we walked a good distance from the landing before we finally arrived at the village around five o'clock that evening. The village was in a valley and the surrounding green hills made it look so beautiful. This was where Mr. Labriel and his family stayed. We all slept there for the night.

On the following morning, my husband got two men to carry our luggage, and a guide to continue with us to San Antonio. About halfway into the journey, we saw at a distance two very bare hills. Neither tree nor bush, nor grass was on it. He asked one of the Maya men what caused the hill to be like that—being so far in the wilderness.

"*Yo no se quien va quemar este cerro,*" the Maya man answered, meaning that he did not know who burnt that hill.

The large clearing with the new tiny growth of plants which we noticed as we got nearer, showed that it must have been a really big fire that swept across the hill.

Soon after we started our walk from Aguacate to San Antonio, our guide suggested that it was better to change route and take the short cut over the hills. They said the short cut would take us only about four hours, whereas the trail that we were originally taking through Murphy Die Creek would take more than six hours. As we wanted to arrive home sooner, we took the guide's advice and changed our route.

That decision turned out to be one that we would regret for a long time. We found the mountain route to be very dangerous and very hard to climb. There were many sharp and loose rocks on it. Some sections were steep upward climbs and we had to take each step very carefully. Any slip would be a deadly fall way below. We also had to make sure that as we walked we did not cause loose rocks to fall on the person climbing behind us. I couldn't understand how anybody could walk over these hills or how the Maya guides walked them so swiftly and fearlessly. Several times along the way we had to rest so we could catch our breath. After that journey whenever anybody came to San Antonio and looked south at the big mountains there, we recalled having climbed them already. We have left our footprints all over those places.

## *Garifuna Wood-cutters Visit San Antonio*

A few weeks after we arrived in San Antonio, two of our Garifuna countrymen dropped by to visit. They were woodcutters passing through from Aguacate where they had been searching for mahogany. Since it was getting late in the evening they dropped by to visit. Mr. Enriquez and I were especially glad to see them since we rarely see our countrymen in this area. We welcomed the men to stay with us for the night as they were very tired and hungry. While they rested for a while in the extra hammocks we tied for them, I prepared dinner.

In those days many of our Garifuna men worked as woodcutters in lumber camps all over the hinterlands of the district. These two worked for the mahogany contractor Mr. William Bourne from Punta Gorda. There were other contractors in Punta Gorda such as Mr. W. T. Watrous, Serriano Lambey, Sidney Perret and Thomas Moore who also had Garifuna men working for them. Around that time woodcutting was a very big business and a lot of mahogany, rosewood and other woods were shipped from Punta Gorda to Belize and from there to other countries.

These strong, muscular Garifuna woodcutters who were visiting our home that evening turned out to be very funny and lighthearted. After they finished eating their meal, they talked a lot about their experiences travelling through the forests in their search of mahogany, their way of surviving the jungle, and about their families that they leave for long periods of time at home in Punta Gorda. From them I learnt so much about their way of life.

That evening they also shared many stories that filled us with laughter. One of the stories they related was an experience that had happened to them in Aguacate. When they arrived in that village after a long hard day in the forest, they sought lodging for the night at the home of one of the natives and were received cordially. While they were seated, they saw the mistress of the house walking lively up and down by the fire hearth, at the farther end of the house. One of the men noticed that the same lady took a chamber pot, set it on the fire hearth and poured water into it for boiling tea. In another chamber pot she was cooking some food.

Seeing this, he began to get worried and uneasy over the matter and whispered to his companion who was looking outside, "Gee-weez man, just look there. It seems as though that woman is going to cook for us in the chamber-pot. Heavens sake! That has never happened to me since I came out of my mother's womb!"

His partner just took it easy and explained, "Relax! These people are not like us. They do not use that pot to poo in; they buy it only for cooking purposes."

The woodcutters also shared another funny experience that they had on their way to San Antonio. It happened that night had caught them along the trail. Luckily their dog had caught a gibnut earlier just before sun down. After they had climbed to the top of the hill, they set up camp and then skinned and cooked the gibnut. While they were eating the meat they felt that some parts were tough and other parts tender and nice. They did not know what caused this especially because they couldn't see in the dark. They had no lamp or flashlight and saw only by the light of the fire. After supper they went to bed.

The following morning they woke up and lit the fire to warm the meat that was left over. After it was warm enough, they uncovered the pot and dished out the food. When they began to eat, they noticed that there were two kinds of meat in the plates. On closer examination they found the meat of a big frog cut up into several bits and mixed with the gibnut meat. They had felt very badly about eating that stew and even wanted to throw away the remaining portion that was left in the pot. However the elder of them advised that since they had both enjoyed the stew the night before and got no stomach illness or anything, and had even slept soundly, it must have been a good meal. Instead of throwing away the entire stew, they decided to throw away only the pieces of frog meat and eat the gibnut.

The lively way in which they told each story was such a capital joke to us that we could not help but burst with laughter. Since the nights in the village were always very quiet, our loud laughter late into the night must have been heard a good distance away by villagers who had only been used to the night sounds of crickets or frogs before they retired early to sleep. It was the only time in the village that we had such a visit by our countrymen.

The following morning after we shared breakfast, both men left in their happy mood to continue their search for mahogany. There must have been something about their work roaming the forest and camping wherever night caught them, which made these woodcutters so lively, funny and lighthearted.

## *Christmas Holidays 1913-14*

The school term went by smoothly without incident and as Christmas was drawing near again and we decided to spend the holidays at home in Punta Gorda. It was arranged that this time we return by the Moho River route as the Punta Gorda route was always in muddy and swampy condition during this season.

A few days before we were to travel, Mr. Enriquez reminded the alcalde about the agreement that was made with the priest and us to assist in our travel back to Punta Gorda for vacation. The agreement was that the alcalde would hire two men and horses to assist in carrying our luggage.

Quite disappointingly, on the morning of our travel, however, the men all refused to go despite all the coaxing. We waited until almost midday hoping they would change their minds but none of them appeared. Quite often we had experienced that many of the Mayas were not very reliable in living up to their promises. Once these promises were broken it was very difficult to have them change their minds no matter how we tried to reason with them. My husband had to quickly make other travel arrangements and pay for our own expenses. This time we left by way of the Murphy Die Creek and reached the village of Aguacate very late that Saturday evening. The following morning, we continued to Punta Gorda.

Being greatly annoyed at this disappointment, Mr. Enriquez refused to go back to reopen the school in San Antonio at the beginning of the new year, January, 1914. He considered quitting his work there. Meanwhile, he started a plantation, and did some fishing and trading to make a living.

In August of that year, however, when World War I broke out, he agreed with the school's management to return to San Antonio. We returned this time through the Rio Grande and through San Pedro Columbia, a new village of about 200 persons that was just being established. One of the persons living there was our Compadre Tezecum, whose children we had stood for as godparents for their baptism when they were living in San Antonio.

The people of San Antonio were very glad to have us back again. Many visited to welcome us and brought us gifts of corn, plantains, beans and other crops. Mr. Enriquez reopened the school and started his work as usual. At a school meeting, he reminded the people about the discouraging incident that had happened and advised them to cooperate better with us as it was they and their children who stand to benefit from the school. Because of the many hardships we suffered in San Antonio, we always looked forward to spending the Christmas vacation at home in Punta Gorda.

## *Alcalde Election in San Antonio*

One day in 1915, the alcalde notified the people that there was to be an election for this post since his term of office was up. The alcalde, an elected leader of the village, is responsible for law and order. It is he who gathers the men for *fajina*, which is a day when all men participate in clearing the village trails or doing any other community tasks that are required. The alcalde is also the local judge. Whenever there are cases of misbehaviour and crime in the village, the alcalde has the power to hear the case, set a fine or even send persons to prison. The election of an alcalde is always done by the men of the village including young men of marriage age, sixteen years, and older. Elections take place inside the *cabildo*, the building where community meetings are held. The name of each new candidate for the post is recommended by the older men only. Only one name is usually suggested and when a name is announced, voting is done by a show of hands. If there is not a majority then another person is proposed.

This time, the election of the alcalde took three days to complete because it was difficult to find another replacement. Each time the villagers came from their meeting, we asked who the new alcalde was and they answered that they had not found any. Every man seemed to have had the desire to be elected, but wouldn't offer himself. The elders would have to propose him. On the third day, Mr. Enriquez's name was proposed and everybody voted for him even though he was not at the meeting. They explained that they did so because even when they elected a native, they still had to ask Mr. Enriquez for advice on many village matters and for assistance with their secretarial duties. Most of the time, the alcalde discussed matters with Mr. Enriquez before making a decision. Because of this, they explained that they could not and did not see why Mr. Enriquez should not be elected as alcalde.

The villagers immediately sent for Mr. Enriquez asking him to join their meeting at the cabildo. As soon as he arrived, they told him about their decision. However, he declined, explaining that for this position it was best that the alcalde should always be living the village. He further explained that he could not remain in the village during the holidays due to the many hardships that we faced, but that he was quite willing to continue to give the leaders all the necessary help that they needed. He thanked them very much for their high regard for him and went on to say that if it had not been that he had to leave the village during each vacation, he would willingly accept the post.

In reply to all this, the villagers explained that they could let the second Alcalde act when he, the first, was away. Again my husband said that this arrangement would not work since he would still be needed if any serious offense such as killing or chopping took place while he was away. Therefore, he could not accept it. As a result, the same alcalde whose term of office was up, had to keep the position for another term.

## Travel by Rio Grande / House in Punta Gorda

By this time I had mastered the Maya language already. I had also become more at home with the people and was learning more of their customs. All this time, there was no trouble, nor disorder amongst the people. Everything was running smoothly. There was only the trouble of difficult transportation. I was often very sad when I gave birth to stillborn babies. Besides, we had very poor food – pepper and salt, corn tortillas, unsweetened porridge. We always spent Christmas and Easter holidays, and the dry weather May vacation at home in Punta Gorda. Except when I was soon to give birth, (when we went home by river) we usually walked from the village all the way home in Punta Gorda.

San Pedro Columbia was by this time becoming more inhabited and a new school became established. Andres Gutierrez, a Garifuna from Punta Gorda now deceased, was the first teacher there. May he rest in peace.

In the year 1916, we managed to rent a furnished house in Punta Gorda to stay in during the school vacation. Before then we stayed with our parents at different times during each school vacation. Because we had nothing to start life by ourselves in Punta Gorda and since we spent most of the year in the village, we spent the holidays of the first two years with my mother, then the next two years with my husband's aunt before repeating this pattern again.

That whole year went quite all right. It became easier to travel by way of Rio Grande. Although the trail that we walked from San Antonio to the departure point at the Rio Grande was several miles through many hills and slippery valleys, it was not as difficult as walking all the way to Punta Gorda. This route to the river only took us about a little over three hours. From there the rest of the journey to Punta Gorda was by dory on the river.

## Peacefully Settling a Village Argument

The earlier part of 1917 also went well. We had no trouble with the people in the village except a minor incident that occurred one evening when a few mothers encouraged their husbands to violently threaten Mr. Enriquez for detaining their children after school hours to get their lessons mastered. I noticed on a number of occasions, that although the people generally looked so humble and calm, the men could easily be influenced to flare up violently and sometimes the women nagged them to react this way when the quarrels involved them. Once in a while these quarrels resulted in men chopping each other, especially when they are drunk. Quite often my husband had to intervene and talk to those involved to prevent this from happening.

That evening when they threatened my husband, he never raised his voice or moved away or showed any fear. Instead, he calmly explained to them that since the world was getting more and more civilized, the school lessons were for their own benefit. He told them that he did not go to the village to waste time. He further gave them practical examples, saying that the children would need to know how to sell their beans or corn by the quart and how to calculate the cost. The villagers used to have much trouble to find out the cost of so many quarts of corn or beans at, for example, ten cents a quart. They had to go to the educated ones to help them to find out the correct price of their products. He told these parents that all his work was being done to enlighten the children and therefore, they should have confidence in him. By the end of his talk, the parents all went back home calmly. Since then, they all cooperated in his work with their children.

As his assistant at school, Mr. Enriquez had Alejandro Ogaldez, the son of Mrs. Alberta Ogaldez. Alejandro was a pupil teacher in San Antonio from January 1917 to January 1918. He was working for $4.00 a month. Before he came to San Antonio, he was a pupil teacher at the Punta Gorda school. He was brought to San Antonio to replace Ciriaco Choc, a native who was dismissed for too much drinking and misbehaving with the pupils. When Alejandro came to San Antonio, John Zuniga took his place in Punta Gorda. After one year Alejandro returned to Punta Gorda and Presentacion Cho, who was 15 years old and a former student of Mr. Enriquez, was hired as the pupil teacher for three years.

## Priest Visits

Once every three or four months the priest visited the village to have Mass, and for baptisms, confessions and marriages. Once a year, the Bishop visited for confirmation. In between these visits Mr. Enriquez had prayer services or funeral services. At school he also taught the children to sing the church hymns in Latin. It was always good to see how beautifully they sang in different voices after he spent a lot of time training them. Some of the students found it very difficult to sing in Latin but with extra practice they learned.

Mr. Enriquez often joked that at one of his singing classes there was a particular student who was singing so badly that he asked, "Are you singing or are you talking?"

"I am singing teacher," the shy student murmured.

Eventually after much training and practice that student became one of the best singers and this made her very proud of herself.

When the school holidays began again, we were home bound. Since there was nowhere to sleep along the way, and the weather was very good, we had to move fast enough to try to cover the dry San Antonio—Punta Gorda trail within the same day. That was such a painful physical strain on us that after we arrived in Punta Gorda we had to rest for a few days to recover. Apart from that, the May vacation with our families was relaxing, enjoyable and well spent. During this time, my husband sent an application to the District Officer to lease a lot in Punta Gorda.

During the month of June 1917, all the teachers went together as a group to ask Fr. Tenk, the manager, for their May vacation grant. He refused to give it to them, even though from the beginning of his work, Mr. Enriquez and other teachers had been working hard to teach this other race of people. We stayed in Punta Gorda only until Christmas.

In January 1918, we went back to San Antonio to hold over the school until the summer holidays.

## *Influenza at Rancho*

In June 1918, after I completed six years in San Antonio and my husband completed about eleven years there, we were transferred to Rancho to stay among a different race of people—the East Indians or descendants of Hindus, also locally called Coolies. Rancho was also known as the Toledo Settlement, which was made up of different estates such as Fairview, Westmoreland, Forest Home, Eldorado, Spice Hill, Fern Hill, and the Coleman Estates. Among the East Indians were also a few Spanish and Creole people who were working at the sugar estates. They all lived quite nicely together in the community. We stayed there for the whole month of June.

During the month of July that year, my husband became very ill with a persistent and severe headache, cough, cold and high fever. All his joints were aching and his back was painfully stiff. I believe this was a result of the changing weather conditions he had experienced as he walked through the Pine Ridge area on the trail from San Antonio. During that long strenuous journey under the blazing heat of the sun, a heavy shower suddenly came and he became soaking wet until he shivered under the cool weather. Further along the journey the sunny weather returned and blazed again. Shortly thereafter, however, the dark clouds covered the sky again and the cold shower drenched him until he shivered. These changes between heat and cold on his tired body made him very ill. Because of his illness, he had to take a leave from school and remain at home while he recovered. We could not go down to Punta Gorda until near the end of August, just about two weeks before giving birth.

On September 5, that same year 1918, our first living child Olivia Justiniana was born in Punta Gorda.

News came in September 1918 that the Spanish influenza was raging in Belize. By October, all schools were closed as the influenza was spreading throughout the colony and people were dying everywhere. My husband had not yet fully recovered from the illness he had in July and so his body was not strong enough to resist the flu. He became so much worse that the doctor decided that his case was hopeless. I thought that I would have lost him and buried him, but I made sure to take very good care and nursed him back to good health. Even I myself became sick but I had to force myself to be strong for both the newborn and my sick husband. By the blessing of the Almighty, we both got better.

We were happy to learn in November of that year that my husband's application for the lot that he had sent in almost two years before, was approved. We got the lease to lot number 408 in Punta Gorda.

School did not re-open at Rancho until February 1919. The people all cooperated with Mr. Enriquez in the work of the school. They did well with their children and he continued to give all his best efforts. Some of the Mr. Enriquez's pupils from Rancho who have grown up to become well known businessmen and leaders in their community are Peter Coleman, Henry Williams, Marion Tulcey, Thomas Tulcey, Alexander Ramclam and Dan Jacobs.

## El Cayo de San Ignacio

Around the end of May 1919, we were given short notice by the school management that my husband was to be transferred to El Cayo. He accepted the transfer and immediately we packed our belongings and said our quick goodbyes to family and friends.

We departed Punta Gorda early in June and stayed in Belize for a few days while we tried to find passage to El Cayo. It was on a Saturday morning at about five o'clock that we began our journey to El Cayo in a Belize-Cayo motorboat. It was a very rough trip of about a hundred and thirty miles up the Belize River. Because the rainy season had not quite set in, the river was very low. The boatmen had to use rope, pole and motor to pass over the waterfalls and rapids. Quite often, all the men had to get into the water to help push the boat. We did not arrive in Cayo until Thursday morning.

Shortly after we settled in, Fr. Fenoughty, the school manager, introduced us to the people of El Cayo. The population of the town was about 1,000 persons most of whom were Mestizos and Mayas with some Creoles and a few Syrians. We found everyone to be very friendly. Whenever they dropped by to visit our home they reminded us not to feel like strangers; everybody was treated alike. They invited us visit their homes to make friends, as that was the way they lived. Our occasional visits to their homes earned us some genuine friends and new acquaintances. We lived in the teachers' quarters in the churchyard near the school.

We were pleased with the house where we lived. Unlike the thatched house where we stayed in San Antonio, this one that the mission provided was very comfortable and had all conveniences that was worthy of a teacher and his family to live in. It was the first time in my husband's teaching career that we lived in a good house.

Mr. Enriquez found the children to be very backward in their schoolwork. He had to work hard to give them extra lessons to bring them up to a good level. The children eventually showed great improvement and their parents were very grateful to him.

We were living quite happily at El Cayo and we thought we were going to stay there for a long time. In 1920, the year after we arrived there, Mr. Peter Requena of Santa Elena promised to lease a piece of land from his property to my husband. We planned to use this land to make a plantation in order to ease our family from the high cost of living.

One day, Fr. Fenoughty who heard about my husband's plan asked me, "Why doesn't Mr. Enriquez plan go to Belize and try to obtain a First Class Certificate instead of trying to start a plantation?"

When I mentioned the priest's concern to my husband he answered, "You know, it is the same reason that I am making the plantation. This will help us to cut down on food expenses and to earn a little extra so as to help me afford the trip."

Fr. Joseph Fenoughty, who served in Punta Gorda 1917-1918, was the priest in San Ignacio when the Enriquez family was there.

At that time, all the teachers in the colony had to travel to Belize to take the examination. This was very difficult for them, as they had to pay out of their own pockets for every move. Even when they were transferred to another place, the teachers had to meet all the expenses of transferring their families. This made it

Students of Cayo School when Andres Enriquez was Principal (1919-1921)

more difficult for them to separate themselves from their families to take their exams in Belize City. With their small salaries, they had to find other ways to raise funds.

Later that year, I began to have some doubts about whether or not we would stay in El Cayo for a long time as we had believed. These doubts started in a strange way. The priest had arranged for some building posts to be cut and he informed Mr. Enriquez that these were going to be used for building the new church. We believed this to be true as the church was too old and shabby for a town like El Cayo. The roof was partly thatched and partly metal. The walls were made of lumber and some of the wooden posts seemed to be growing leaves. The church also had a level earthen floor. The bell in front of the church was supported by two posts with a stick placed cross-wise on them from where the bell was suspended. This cracked bell sounded like a half-broken pot. So it was not hard for us and the other people to believe that the posts were for the building of a new church.

One evening after a church service, Fr. Huerman, Miss Blancanuex and I were conversing in front of the church. Forgetting that I was present and what he had mentioned to my husband and me a few weeks before, Fr. Huerman told Miss Blancanuex that he was getting some posts to build a convent for the Sisters who would be brought in to teach at the parish. Immediately after he said this he realized that I was there with them and grew very nervous and uneasy. Seeing him that way, I explained that such a move was to be expected sooner or later.

When I got home, I related the incident to my husband. I told him that we should no longer believe that we were going to stay in the place for a long time, as I had overheard the secret plans that the priest had mistakenly shared. I also told my husband that we should make up our minds to expect to be transferred again soon. He was very disappointed to learn about the plans of the priest. No one had ever told him that the nuns were expected there and that he would soon be transferred.

He then explained, "In such a case, because we are unsure about what is going to happen, there is no use to continue my plan to go to Belize soon. Another transfer coming so soon after all we spent to move from Punta Gorda would only double our expenses."

Despite this uncertainty about our stay, Mr. Enriquez continued to do well at school. The parents cooperated so well and the students were making very good progress. He organized a school entertainment and it was a great success. A large crowd attended and filled the hall to capacity. Everything else that he did at school turned out successful. The parents always cooperated and told us how good they felt about the school's progress and activities. Even the school examination was a big success.

Staying with us at our home, besides our two-year-old daughter Olivia, were Claro Villafranco, my 14-year-old only brother, and Evangelista Apolonio, whose mother was a first cousin of my husband. Both Claro and Evangelista carried on nicely with the native children and became their playmates. Bringing these two older children from Punta Gorda to live with us was a great help. Claro did most of my errands and often went with the other boys to collect firewood. He also went with the boys to bathe in the river or just romped about the community. Evangelista played with the baby while I did my housework. All of us were quite happy at El Cayo. We did not go to Punta Gorda for any of the holidays because Mr. Enriquez wanted to save enough money to afford taking his exam.

Quite often friends, neighbors and others from the community came to our home to visit, and I also walked around returning their visits. There was no trouble at all with the natives. They were very friendly and caring. The priests were Fr. Huerman and Fr. Fenaoughty.

Early in the year 1921, I was greatly exposed with child and in March of the same year Mr. Enriquez received notice that he was to be transferred Progresso Village in the Lowry's Bight Lagoon, via Corozal. Although we had expected that this transfer would have happened soon, he was still disappointed that the priest did not inform him earlier. He had only suspected this transfer after I shared what I had overheard in the priest's conversation a few months earlier. Even then, we weren't completely sure since the priest had made no direct mention about the transfer after I had overheard his plans.

In April, the following month, we started to get ready to leave. Several persons from the community told us during their visits, or when we meet them at church or in the streets or shops, that they were so sorry to learn that we were leaving. Mr. Enriquez and I were also sad to be leaving just when we had been settling in the community so well. Since we could not travel with all the belongings we had gathered there, we sold whatever we could, and whatever remained, we had to give away.

Five days before we were scheduled to leave, the people of El Cayo gave us a grand farewell party. Some of those attending were Messrs. Candelario de la Fuente, Cecil Gray and Charles Louis. There were a number of ladies too. A variety of native food was served including tamales, bollos, and relleno. Mr. Gray played the violin, Mr. Charlie the mandolin and another played a guitar, all of which made heavenly music. It was too bad that due to my pregnant condition, I couldn't dance. Occasionally Mr. Enriquez joined in the dancing. When it was time for his farewell speech, he mentioned that he was sorry to leave so early just when he had gotten so used to working and living among the people. He thanked the people very much for their kindness and all their support and wished them well. All this happened on a Saturday evening.

By the time we were scheduled to leave, the construction of the Sisters' convent had already begun. We finished our packing and were ready to leave El Cayo on Thursday morning. Fortunately and unfortunately, two days before we were due to leave, I gave birth to a baby girl, Zenobia Celestina, on April 26, 1921. Because of this, we had no choice but to remain in the building for two more weeks.

The priests were aware of the inconveniences of my family, having to delay our travel after just having a baby. However, in their hurry to have the accommodations ready for the Pallotine nuns, they were inconsiderate. They did not even offer us another temporary place. The carpenters continued hammering and sawing at the roof and walls almost near my bed as it was from that side that the house was being extended. You can imagine what great inconvenience the baby and I were in, on account of all this. The noise gave me splitting headaches. They did not even care about the baby crying through all the noise they were causing from their work. I thought that the work was going to be held up at least for a little while to accommodate us. It was only by the help of the Almighty that I did not have a blood flow.

Soon after, the baby was baptized and the natives of El Cayo once more gave a dance in her honor. Since we had already sold or given away most of our belongings, and since the mission wanted us out of the place, we had no choice but to travel home to Punta Gorda as soon as possible. The baby was only two weeks old when we took the long journey by the river boat from El Cayo to Belize and then by another boat from Belize to Punta Gorda.

Along the way from El Cayo to Belize, the kind captain and the sailors made extra effort to take very good care of me. They even tied a hammock for me in the motorboat so that I would not have to sit down and get shaken. I was very grateful to them for making my travel more bearable. Throughout most of the journey I remained lying down in the hammock with the baby.

When we arrived in Belize a few days later, we faced another inconvenience—that of finding a place to lodge. I had to remain in the boat for hours with my two-week-old baby, my two-year-old Olivia, the girl Evangelista, and my young brother Claro while my husband walked all around looking for lodging. After searching desperately for a few hours, he finally found a place and came back for us. We stayed in Belize for three days while Mr. Enriquez searched desperately again for passage to proceed to Punta Gorda. There was no space for all of us on the regular boat; every available space was taken.

At long last, the only passage that Mr. Enriquez found to travel to Punta Gorda was on a schooner that traveled to Punta Gorda only now and then. Travelling in these vessels took a longer time than on the regular boat. Since we were quite tired and were suffering a lot of inconveniences at the place where we stayed in Belize, especially in my condition, we were quite glad to get anything to get home. Once in the boat, we spread sheets and towels on the floor as bedding for the children and ourselves and took the long sea journey home.

## *More Sad News in Punta Gorda*

We arrived in Punta Gorda very late that night and this time we did not bother to wait until morning to find our way home. As soon as we landed, we heard the shocking news that Mr. Enriquez's aunt had died while we were at El Cayo. We immediately walked to the home of my husband's other aunt. She was so surprised to see us and to hear that we had traveled so far with our very young children, especially the newborn baby. She embraced us and wept saying that she was so sad about the recent death of her sister and especially that

Archival photos of a street in Cayo and the boats used for travel to Cayo that the Enriquez family would have used. Note the hammock in the center photo.

Passenger boat, E.M.L., at the pier in Punta Gorda, 1917. This boat was the main source of transportation from Punta Gorda to Belize City in the early 1900s.

Punta Gorda sea front in the 1940s.

Siblings, Solomon and Zenobia Enriquez served as godparents at the baptism of Mayan children, photo taken in 1942.

Wedding of Zenobia Enriquez (1) at St. Peter Claver Church, Punta Gorda, to John Palacio, Sr. (2) Other family members attending included: Olivia Enriquez (3), Andres Enriquez (4), Jane V. Enriquez (5), Solomon (6), and Elicia (7).
(*numbers above and to the right of the indicated person*)

her nephew (my husband) did not have the happiness of seeing his aunt and brother alive again. We lodged at her house that night and on the following day we went to our own home.

Mr. Enriquez's only brother Sylverio had also passed away while we were in El Cayo. He died on November 14, 1920, after a sudden illness and was buried the following day at the cemetery in Punta Gorda. At his death Sylverio left behind his wife Mrs. Marcelina Enriquez nee Avilez, who was about seven months pregnant, and their five sons—Camilo, Reyes, Lucio, Basilio and Charles. Martin Alfred Enriquez, the baby we met with her, was born two months after his father died. Fr. Tenk was the priest back then.

In times like these we realize how very hard it was to be far away from our family and not hear about the death or burial of loved ones until long afterwards.

As usual, my mother and sister and all my relatives were so glad to see us in good health with our new stranger, the three-week-old baby Zenobia. My husband, the children and I spent the whole month of May 1921 together in Punta Gorda. Around that time the population of Punta Gorda was about 900 persons, most of whom were Garifuna with only a few Creole and Spanish families.

## *Progresso Village*

Early in June 1921, Mr. Enriquez travelled alone to his new station, Progresso. I had to stay in Punta Gorda a bit longer because the baby was too young to take that long journey all the way from there all the way up to Corozal. We had no idea what it would be like to travel to Progresso with young children. Therefore he and I agreed that it was best that he went ahead to find and prepare a place for us to stay.

It was not until the end of August when the baby was four months old that I traveled from Punta Gorda to join him again. My mother had asked my fifteen-year-old brother Claro Joseph to accompany me and the two babies—two-year-old Olivia and four-month-old Zenobia—on this long trip. After the farewell hugs that my mother, sisters and other family members gave us at the Punta Gorda pier that bright morning, we departed on the motorboat, Lily C.

The sea was quite calm as we traveled from Punta Gorda to Monkey River Town, Placencia and Sittee. At each of these places the boat stopped for about half an hour or so to offload and pick up cargo and people. I enjoyed looking at the calm scenery along the way. As we traveled further north towards Dangriga, however, the light breeze became stronger and stronger until it blew heavily all along the way from Newtown to Dangriga. The wind became so strong and the waves so rough near Dangriga that the vessel rocked from side to side. Some people even fell out of their bunk beds to the floor.

As the night wore on, the wind became even stronger and stronger. Then came the heavy rains, thunder and lightning. The storm rocked the boat so strongly that I strained myself all night trying to keep in position. With one hand I grabbed tightly on a beam and with the other I held the baby tightly. When the boat leaned to one side, I tried to pull back and when it leaned on the other side, I pressed down the opposite side. I could not sleep that night as I tried desperately to maintain balance. I kept praying that the storm would go quickly. It was a good thing that Claro was with me to help take care of the older baby. The stormy weather continued until we arrived in Belize extremely tired at about four o'clock in the morning.

The children and I lodged in Belize for two days before I could find another passage to Corozal Town in the sailing vessel E.M.L. The trip from Belize to Corozal was also very uncomfortable. The heat during that day caused my baby, Zenobia, to cry very much. Even when I suckled her she would not be quieted. By the time night set in, the baby and I must have been so tired that I didn't even realize when we both fell fast asleep. However, I was awakened by a very cool land breeze that blew on my head and this, after the very hot weather during the day, gave me severe neuralgia.

As soon as our boat arrived in Corozal Town, the passengers were met at the pier by the medical officer, the customs officer, and health officers. They all explained that all passengers and the crew were to remain in Corozal Town and that no one was to leave to any other destination. Because there was an outbreak of the infectious Yellow Fever disease in Belize City where we had come from, they had to first make sure that no one was infected.

A little later that morning the motorboat from Progresso arrived to pick up the children and me as Mr. Enriquez had arranged. Since

I was eager to get to Progresso early and settle in after such long traveling, I went to look for the doctor to try to convince him that my children and I were alright and to ask his permission to leave Corozal. Unfortunately the doctor wasn't at the clinic so I explained my case to the Nurse. I explained to her that it would be very inconvenient me to stay in Corozal Town alone with the children after traveling all the way from Punta Gorda to join my husband who was teaching in Progresso. Since the boat that my husband chartered had already come all the way from Progresso to pick me up, it would be better for the children and me to continue our journey. The nurse was very understanding and she granted me permission to leave.

We sailed away from Corozal Town later that morning and arrived in Progresso in the afternoon, shortly after school was over for the day. Mr. Enriquez gladly came to meet us at the pier with a few school children and men to help us carry our luggage to our home. I felt such a relief and joy to finally arrive at my new home after all that rough travelling with the children all the way from Punta Gorda It was so good to be with my husband again.

However, the joy of arrival was quickly disturbed by some trouble. As soon as we were about to unpack and settle in, the village policeman arrived at our home and ordered Mr. Enriquez to immediately return the children and me to Corozal Town. I tried desperately to explain that the Nurse had granted me permission to travel but since I had no admission papers as proof, he did not change his mind. There were strict laws to make sure that the outbreak of Yellow Fever in Belize did not spread to the other parts of the colony. I felt very, very disappointed but we had to follow their orders. Immediately the boat returned with us to Corozal Town. Mr. Enriquez also came along to try to sort out the situation.

Soon after we arrived in Corozal Town that night, the officials sent a telegram to Belize asking permission for me to go Progresso since they found no kind of illness on me.

The reply to the telegram took long in coming. Because Mr. Enriquez had only a day and a half leave from the school manager, he had to return to Progresso without the children and me before the time of his leave expired. We felt very disappointed that he had to return alone as there was nothing we could do but wait for the permission from the health authorities in Belize.

Quite happily, I received notice of the telegram granting permission for me to travel to Progresso; but sadly, when it came my husband had just departed. I rushed to the pier hoping that the boat had delayed a bit and that I could still catch it. By that time I got there, however, the boat had just departed. From the dock, I waved my hands desperately just in case one of the passengers looked back and see me. That did not happen. Tears rolled down my cheeks as I gazed at the boat getting smaller and smaller until it disappeared in the distance. If only I could have called the boat back, I would have done so.

After a very long trip from Punta Gorda, I was then stranded in Corozal Town as a complete stranger with my young children. We stayed there for a whole long week and managed with assistance from the Head teacher who found us temporary lodging with members of the church. It was a very rough time and I had to have a lot of patience not knowing when I would find another boat passage. In those days, it was very difficult to find a passage to Progresso. There was also no way to send a message to inform my husband. After his recent expense of chartering a boat, it was too much for him to pay for another charter to pick us up not knowing when we would receive the permission. Taking out more time from school under this uncertainty was another difficulty. Luckily, however, my brother Claro was very mature and very helpful. Long at last, the children and I returned to Progresso and settled. Claro did not stay; he returned to Punta Gorda soon after to find work.

At first I did not like Progresso. I found the place to be very lonely especially during the day when my husband went to school, leaving me alone in the big house with the two little children. Whenever I peeped out of the house I didn't see anybody; only hogs, turkeys and fowls and some goats that strayed around the village. After experiencing the liveliness of the people of El Cayo, I felt really lost during my first few months in Progresso. The inhabitants seemed slow to make friends. Furthermore, I became very sickly. In fact, during the entire eight years that we lived in Progresso, there was not a month that passed in which I did not become ill with a cold, cough, or some other illness, and I believe this was because of the lagoon climate, which probably did not agree with my health.

Our new house was fairly large in size and very comfortable. I liked the convenience of the big kitchen. The yard outside was also unusually big, as it was comprised of double lots. In the backyard were pear, plum, mammie apple, breadnut and coconut trees. My husband and I made the backyard into our own little plantation. There we planted plantains, bananas, cacao, and sugarcane for our home use. We also made an extra garden where we planted tomatoes, beans, habanero pepper and corn. The other section of the yard that was not planted was used as an area for raising our turkeys and chickens. We were quite happy to get so much of our food from what we planted or raised in our backyard.

The water that we first used from the well was bad and we had no vat. Later, we used empty drums to collect water when it rained. Otherwise, when the weather was dry we fetched water from a vat at the home of Mr. Gabino Olivera. Mr. Olivera was a chiclero contractor and one of the rich men of the village. He was also a wholesale and retail dealer in groceries, dry goods and liquor. When his vat was half empty, we had to fetch water from the wells. There were some wells where the water could not even be used for cooking or for washing our clothes. In general, the people had to use ashes for washing and so the clothes wore out very fast.

Through the challenges of settling in this new community, we made ourselves at home. It was there that I mastered Spanish. While Mr. Enriquez and the older children went to school, I kept myself busy with my duties in the house, with the babies and about the yard with the plants and chickens. The school was a fair distance away from the house where we lived.

It was interesting for me to notice that the people of Progresso had old-fashioned ways of dressing. The women wore long skirts and morning jackets, while the girls had simple plain coloured skirts and a kind of midway blouse and simple slippers as footwear. The men wore pants and undershirts as their daily wear but when they dressed, they wore shirts and sometimes a jacket.

It was also surprising to me that the people of the village were divided and did not relate well with one another. One half of the village was against the other half for no good reason at all. Sometimes they quarreled and at other times they just ignored each other. I learned that for a number of years, long before we arrived, the people had been divided along racial lines with the Mulattos and the "colored people" on one side, and the Mestizos on the other. Both sides earned money from mahogany and chicle extraction.

This division showed in many ways. For example, Mr. Gabino Olivera, the store owner and chiclero contractor, and who was the representative of the whole village, had his own orchestra of musicians while Mr. Ruperto Pasos, a former teacher, also had his own. No one from either group went to the dance of the other.

Because of this division of proud and quarrelsome people in the village, it was very hard at first for Mr. Enriquez and me to make friends. Each group wanted us to be seen as supporting its side and each of them spoke badly against the other. It was a challenge for us to try not to be seen as favoring one side over the other. Mr. Enriquez and I, having heard both sides, explained to each of them that we didn't go to their village to serve half the people only; we went to serve all. We advised each party that it was not a good thing for their village to be divided but rather it was better to live as one, for unity is strength. We also kept reminding them that they were such a wonderful people to be acting that way.

In 1922, a small family of three sisters came to Progresso to settle and look for a livelihood. The sisters, Petty, Evelyn and Maggie Burns, became our neighbours and we found them to be very good Christian people. One day Mr. Enriquez suggested to Miss Maggie Burns that if she would like to take up teaching he would introduce her to the school manager since there was a need for an assistant. She agreed to try and immediately Mr. Enriquez wrote to the manager in Corozal Town. The response of her acceptance came quickly and she gladly started teaching with great interest in her new career. She co-operated with Mr. Enriquez and did whatever she was told.

The agreement we had made with the school management for staying at the mission house was that I would cook for the priest whenever he visited the village. That was what I did for those eight years that we were in Progresso. The priest used to visit every three months or so and stayed for a few days. I used to take very good care of him as well as the Bishop and other church visitors, even though I had my household duties to carry out. I did whatever it took to make sure that they ate well and that their meals were served on time.

Once I got a girl from the village to help me take care of my babies while I sponsored the village nurse and another girl for their Confirmation. As soon as Confirmation Mass was over, I served dinner to Bishop Hopkins and the other visitors before carrying my *hijada* or godchild to her home. Sometimes I felt quite upset when the visitors departed because I got so used to taking care of them during their stay. I got to miss them and look forward to their coming back.

That was why I became very sad when I heard the shocking news of the sudden death of Bishop Fredrick Hopkins in early April 1923. I used to serve his meals whenever he visited and enjoyed his kindness and friendliness to our family. Bishop Hopkins, along with

Most Rev. Frederick Hopkins, S.J.
Second Bishop of Belize 1899-1923

two Sisters of Mercy and many other passengers drowned when the E.M.L., which was overloaded with cargo and people, sank off the coast of Sarteneja along its way to Corozal. The EML was the same old cargo boat in which I had first traveled to Corozal.

Shortly after we heard the news of Bishop Hopkins' death, Mr. Enriquez received instructions to close the school for a day in the Bishop's honor. All other schools in the colony also closed that same day. Mr. Enriquez spent part of that day leading prayers with the people in honour of our dear Bishop who was head of our church for more than 23 years. With my two young children, Olivia four years old, and Zenobia two years old, I joined the people at the prayer services.

After the death of Bishop Hopkins, it took several months until much later the following year before Bishop Joseph Murphy, the new Bishop, visited the village.

Most Rev. Joseph A. Murphy, S.J.
Third Bishop of Belize, 1924-1938

The E.M.L., which was a main source of transport along the coast of Belize, sank on April 10, 1923 off the coast of Sarteneja, within seven miles of Corozal Town, resulting in loss of lives of eighteen persons, including Roman Catholic Bishop Fredrick Charles Hopkins. With the exception of the bishop, the passengers who drowned were all women and children. The E.M.L., reportedly overloaded with seventy-one passengers and cargo, sank within ten minutes after filling with water from a leak.

In the year 1923 also, Mr. Enriquez and his assistant, Miss Maggie, planned to organize a school entertainment. He asked Miss Maggie to go around seeking for a few mature and intelligent girls whose parents would allow them to take part in the school play. The parents were in favour of the idea and so the teachers started rehearsing with the children. After each practice period, Mr. Enriquez walked with a lantern to leave each of these big girls at their homes, as there were no flashlights then. Seeing this, the people started to have more confidence in us and became friendlier. We began to feel more at home among our friends. Sometimes our friends visited us at our home and at other times we all gathered at their homes.

In August of that same year the government appointed Mr. Enriquez to be a Deputy Registrar in charge of registering births, marriages and deaths in the area. In that same year, the village leaders asked Mr. Enriquez to help them write a letter to petition Governor Hutson to build a telephone office in the village, like the one in Caledonia and other villages. About forty members of the village and Mr. Enriquez signed the petition. However, they were all disappointed at the reply from the Governor that the telephone could not be put there because it would be too expensive. But the villagers said that they would not give up and would try again until they get the phone.

When the time came for the school entertainment, Mr. Enriquez invited both music bands to play so as not to take sides with any of the divided groups in the village. A big enramada dancing shed was set up in front of Mr. Olivera's house and there was a large crowd. The schoolroom was too small to hold that number of spectators. Now to start with, the teachers had to get everything ready. They collected money to buy cloth for making a stage curtain and some boards for building a stage. The people co-operated with Mr. Enriquez in whatever he asked them to do.

The schoolroom was just an open hall with desks and benches. Mr. Enriquez used all the entertainment money to get a good stage built in the schoolroom. From time to time, the money made from each entertainment was used to buy the needs of the school like cupboard, benches and other things. Some men were also paid fifty cents a day to plaster the outer walls of the school so that it could look more decent. The school had about 60 pupils.

By this time, we continued to feel more at home with the people and this was how we gained their confidence. We did very little visiting of homes. Instead of being entertained, we preferred to entertain visitors especially as we knew that we were going to stay among them for a long period of time. The longer we stayed, the more acquainted we became with the people.

During each school holiday, Mr. Enriquez used to organize different kinds of fun activities for the school children. For example, he organized picnics, races or outdoor games. The picnics were held at Little Belize, a small settlement where Mr. Willie Hulse, the mahogany contractor, had his mahogany work. The children were carried in the motorboats. The parents usually prepared their favorite sweets from some young coconuts. Mr. Hulse was always glad to receive the children and offered them treats of lemonade, sweet biscuits and sugarplums. He then played the gramophone for them to dance. Some of the children who had not heard a gramophone before tried to see "the man singing inside."

Although I often longed to go on one of those picnics with the other parents, I could not; I had to stay at home with my little children. Only the teachers and some other adults went with the school children. When the children returned home, they were all lively and looked refreshed. We noticed that such pleasure trips helped the children to study hard, learn better and quicker, and also enlivened them on a whole.

On another occasion, Mr. Enriquez organized a dory race. On the day of the race he was kept busy marking the shallow parts of the water. There was one man in each dory to give the signal. Some people stood on the shore cheering and waving to the racers to encourage them to go faster. Some of them almost fell into the water doing so. You could have seen the boys kneeling in their dories paddling so fast that they looked like little motors, trying all their best to get their dory to win. We, the spectators on the lagoon shore, were quite beside ourselves with laughter at the fun of the sight. The band was also there playing music.

Greasy pole was another form of recreation that Mr. Enriquez organized with the people of the village. The pole was extended from the pier out to the lagoon and greased. At the end of the pole, a bag with wine, ham and money was tied. That part of the lagoon over where the pole extended was deep enough to prevent the boys from getting hurt by the stones or other things when they fell in. When the music gave the signal to begin the competition, each of the boys who took turns to try to walk the full length of the pole looked as if he was in a circus. As they walked the slippery pole, they waved their hands outwards and rocked from foot to foot trying to balance themselves. At first each boy hardly made a few steps before he fell into the water. After a long time, one of them managed to get the reward. The crowd cheered and the band played a two-step tune to felicitate the winners.

Other games that Mr. Enriquez organized were needle race, sack race, egg and spoon race, eating race, shoe race (blindfolded, one takes off his or her shoes, laces it and run to the finish line) barrel race, and placing the missing tail on the picture of a donkey while blindfolded. It was such a joke to see the donkey's tail far from its place, either at the nose, at the side, or the foot, or far away from the body. There was also tug-of-war with the men, especially during the 10th September celebrations.

Since we were so far away from home in Punta Gorda, and because of the inconvenience and expense of traveling with the children, we could not go there to spend the holidays as often as we would like; we had to remain in Progresso. Holiday time in Progresso was also the time when my husband did more duties at home. He took care of the garden in our yard, planted lots of different types of food crops and fruits for home use and took care of the chickens and turkeys. This is what he used to do when we were in San Antonio or wherever we stayed for a long time. Sometimes he went out fishing with some of the men from the village, casting nets and catching bocotora — turtle.

After three years of remaining in the village, we decided to go and spend the holidays with our family in Punta Gorda. It was always a happy and refreshing break to be with our family in Punta Gorda and to catch up with what was going on with them.

On our way back from Punta Gorda that year, we had to stay unexpectedly in Belize for a whole week, as there was no direct transportation to Progresso. After a week, the boat to Progresso arrived. We started our journey early one morning. After some hours we reached Laguna Seca in the Cocos Lagoon. The tide there had become so low that that the boat could not proceed. We had to wait there bearing the hot rays of the sun for more than half day with the poor children until the high tide came. It was not until around two or three o'clock in the afternoon that the sea breeze blew and the water got high enough for us to continue our journey. At long last, we arrived home quite tired after the long sitting in the boat.

Elicia, my third living child, was the first to be born at Progresso. She was born on June 14, 1923. Then came Solomon, my first son, who was born on February 25, 1925. He was baptized in Belize City during one of our stopovers there on our way to Punta Gorda.

When Elicia was three years old, something very unusual and frightening happened; this changed her whole life. One day in the month of May as I was returning from the kitchen to the main house, I saw the little girl lying on the floor, sleeping. I took her up and put her to bed and found out that she had a very high fever. She sweated out all the fever during that night and looked much better that morning. On the following day almost at the same hour, however, she had a fever again but this time she didn't sweat it out that night. On the following morning, she told me that she wanted to go into the hammock.

She had already learned to walk and talk and was a very sensible child for her age. She was one year and eight months old when Solomon was born. By the time she was two years old, she could rock the baby in his little hammock calling him "Baby Tamaman." She was the little nurse when Olivia and Zenobia went to school for I didn't care to get another village girl to help in the house, as they also had to go to school. I used to have a hard time in that place especially when I got sick far away from home.

That morning I went to the kitchen to prepare some kind of drink for her. While I was in the kitchen, my neighbour came over as usual greeting and inquiring into the health of the family. As she was yet speaking the older children open the door wide with the poor sick child there in the hammock. On seeing this, I went at once to close the door but by the time I got to the girl to give her something to drink, she was in a very bad condition. Every part of her body was trembling.

I got frightened and from the kitchen I called out to my neighbour, "Hay Senora Lina venga a ver a mi chiquita. Yo no se que es lo que le está pasando!"

I wanted Senora Lina to come and see the child since I did not know what was happening to her.

She rushed inside my house and after staring at the child she said, "*Ay maestra! Esta chiquita va a tener ataque.*"

Two hours did not elapse when Elicia had seizures off and on for three days. Afterwards, she had very strong fever for ten consecutive days and ten nights. We tried all we could to get her to sweat it out but all was in vain. Moreover, the doctor was far out of reach. It was too long a distance to go to Corozal as there was too much draught. There were also the other babies that I had to take care of. Besides, there were our school children, Olivia and Zenobia, who could not yet take care of themselves.

Being so far away from my parents and the rest of my family, I then felt very helpless. Although I did not have my father living, I still had my mother, sisters, aunt and uncle at home. Oh, how very different it would be if I were there with them! However, we had friends and neighbours visiting us and they brought herbal medicine that they thought would do some good. You could have smelled all kinds of herbs in our bedroom. While I entertained the visitors my stomach roared with hunger.

All of the visitors gave me consolation saying, "*Dios es grande. Ella va a alivear.*"

Everybody was confused about what kind of medicine was best. Some gave the child hot medicines and others gave her cold medicines. I myself was puzzled for I didn't know anything about medicine or healing as I know now and so I left her in their hands. Even when our neighbour put a hot compress on her feet to draw out the fever, she did not sweat it out.

I went out to call the midwife to see what she could do about the hot, roasting fever. The midwife placed some hot medicines on the child's head and then took it out to put a cold one. Instead the fever on her head rose so high that my poor little daughter became crazy and dumb. This really puzzled me a lot for the child looked terrible. Everybody was frightened to see her in that state and they all sympathized with me. Many times I cried out my sorrow very bitterly.

When Elicia's godmother, Mrs. Olivera, came to the house, she recommended a certain bush doctor named Mr. Agustin Cawich of Pembroke Hall, whose reputation as an herbalist was well known as being the best in the area. How very glad we were to hear about him as we wanted to do anything to make our child well.

Immediately, Mr. and Mrs. Olivera sent for Mr. Cawich and by the following morning, he arrived in Progresso to start his work. When he got to my house, I hardly believed whether this man was really as good as people claimed. He looked so ordinary and simple. He was barefooted and wore a common shirt and pants, and an ordinary straw hat. Because of this, I became doubtful about him. Mr. Cawich looked at the child as I nursed her in my arms and he declared that it was the draught that struck her so badly that she might not live. He assured me, however, that he would cure her because he had cured worse cases than that. I was slightly convinced by his explanation for it was hard to believe such a man especially in such a case.

A little later that morning, following his search around the village, Mr. Cawich returned with about six broad bush leaves. He told my husband to sit down on the box and nurse the sick. He then started his work. First, he took two of the leaves, put them in the form of a cross, placed these on Elicia's head and recited a long prayer in his own language. When he had finished praying with the first two leaves, he did the same with the second two leaves, and then with the third, thereby praying over three crosses. By the time his prayers ended, the patient was fast asleep, as she had not slept much until that time. It was a good thing that she slept; for in that way, I could have also taken a rest in order to gain strength to continue my house work and attend to all the other family members, especially the sick child.

On the following day before Mr. Cawich returned to his home, he came again to see the patient and was glad to see that she was a little improved. He told my husband to go with him to get some more bush medicine. As soon as they entered the bush, Mr. Cawich started plucking a certain type of leaf until they had gone far into the woods. After they had collected sufficient leaves, Mr. Cawich explained that we should boil half of the amount of leaves that they gathered and then bathe the child with this herbal water that is not too hot or too cold. This treatment must be repeated the next day with the other half of the amount of leaves.

The first bath seemed to turn out successful. However, shortly after the poor child became so ill that she trembled like coconut leaves vibrating in the wind. After she took the second bath, she was quiet but looked senseless and completely lost. Her feet were cold and she could not hold anything with her hands. She urinated herself, just like a little baby. I had to nurse both her and baby Solomon, just like twins.

Over time I started to use my home remedies and did whatever the people told me to do. First I cooled her head and put her feet into hot water to bring down the heat from her head. Afterwards, I bathed her with other types of leaves. Some of the natives also pinched her head with a kind of instrument called *"bentosa,"* while I knelt down and prayed and petitioned to the Sacred Heart of Jesus to grant her recovery.

After a few months, she was able to sit up, then crawl and finally walk. On the longer run it was Solomon the younger child who also had to take care of her. Whenever I used to think about what Elicia had gone through, I would cry bitterly. It was very hard for me to bear seeing this child who was so intelligent get to that condition.

Elicia remained dumb for eight months until one day I heard her say her first word, "Papa." When I heard this, I knelt down to give thanks to the Almighty praising Him for His wonderful work. Almost four months elapsed before she said "Mama." I again knelt down to give thanks and did so each time for every word she spoke.

Now, although Elicia is simple-minded, she has mastered four languages fairly well—English, Spanish, Maya and Garifuna—just like all the rest of us in the family. This was a wonderful work of Christ. If at the time of her illness I had the strong faith that I have now, I would have asked Him to cure her completely. Around that time, I myself had also gotten seriously ill twice that I had to go to the Corozal Town hospital to seek treatment. It was very hard for a sick mother to travel with her children.

During all that time, Miss Maggie Burns had become qualified enough to run a school on her own and so she was transferred to Chunux. Mr. Enriquez then trained Miss Maggie's sister Evelyn to take her place in Progresso. However, Evelyn had only worked for six months when she got married to one of the villagers and stopped teaching. Mr. Enriquez then started to train one of his pupils, Anselmo Garcia. However, Anselmo didn't like the job and worked for just a short period. He stopped working despite Mr. Enriquez urging him to keep on. I don't remember if my husband trained one of the grown-up village girls to assist him afterwards.

These were the events that took place during the years from 1921 to 1926.

In the year 1927, on June 29, Peter Louis my second son was born in Progresso. Peter was only two months old when his father got sick with severe dysentery. Because of my husband's illness, school had to be closed while he stayed at home for two weeks trying all sorts of medicine. Despite all this, he got worse and he had to travel to the Corozal Town to be admitted in the hospital. Unfortunately, I could not go with him because our baby was too young; moreover, there were the other children.

Before daybreak, Compadre Olivera helped him to the boat. It was a sad morning for me to see him going alone with good friends, while I did not know whether or not he would return home to me and my children. Two weeks passed and I did not hear anything about him—whether he was still alive or dead. Moreover, there was no passage from here to Corozal. I began to worry a lot and many nights I cried alone as I wondered what would happen if he died, how I would manage alone with the children, and how I would get out of this place with them.

Finally, to the surprise of everybody, Mr. Enriquez returned in the boat from Corozal Town but looking very weak and skinny. He told me all that happened to him during his stay at the hospital. He explained that he had to go on a diet in order to get better since he was far-gone. After he had spent a full week at the hospital, nobody could understand what he said because he was too weak to speak clearly. He was getting only milk and water, then one egg a day with the milk and water, day after day and night after night. Those who went to visit him at the hospital offered him different kinds of foods, but he did not accept these because of the strict diet that the hospital had placed him on.

At the hospital Mr. Enriquez often felt tempted by the food that was served to the other patients. Whenever he saw the ward maid bringing a tray of nice food to the room, he would say to himself, "Now I am going to enjoy some nice dinner today."

Instead, the ward maid only passed by his bed. As he watched her passing by, he swallowed hard at nothing. So hungry he was.

After several days, the doctor tested him by giving him some beef for dinner. He practically swallowed it whole.

After he related his experience at the hospital, I told him that had I been there to see him in that condition, I wouldn't have been able to bear it.

After two weeks as a patient at the hospital, Mr. Enriquez was discharged. The doctor advised him not to drink any kind of alcoholic beverage and not to eat anything contrary to his diet. However, when he left the hospital he felt so weak as though the wind could send him flying like a kite. He went straight to a restaurant and ordered a big dish of tomato soup and a large fish but nothing else, since he still had to be careful. After he had eaten that, he felt his blood become warmer and he felt stronger. At the restaurant, many friends offered him wine and brandy but he refused. All his friends in Corozal Town were surprised to see him so skinny.

The School Manager in Corozal Town advised Mr. Enriquez to take an additional two-week leave to rest before resuming duties and this he did. The people of Progresso were also surprised to see that he had lost so much weight. Compadre Olivera remarked that he had never seen Mr. Enriquez so skinny and that two weeks would not be sufficient for him to rest; he needed more time. I tried all my best to nourish him. By the time the two weeks was over, he was well and strong enough to resume schoolwork. From that time on, my husband did not get sick in Progresso again. Everything returned to normal again and continued so for the entire year.

In May 1928, I became homesick. I had never left Progresso since the year before my husband had gotten ill. I felt out of spirits and lonely from being away from my people for such a long time. Even though I had made friends with some very good people, there were always those times when I thought a lot about my family back in Punta Gorda and how hard it was to stay in touch with them all the way from here. We were at the opposite end of the country; with Punta Gorda being at the extreme south and Progresso being way up north.

During the school holidays, the urge to return home to Punta Gorda with my children was so strong that all my dreams were about home. Because of all that had happened to our family, my husband also talked a lot about wanting to return home. Although the people were very kind to us, my husband and I both shared the same feeling of being at least closer to home with our families. Being away from our relatives and families for so long was hard for us but with more children added to our family, travelling was becoming too expensive. Second class boat passage from Corozal to Belize was $2.50 each and from Belize to Punta Gorda was $3.00 each. Each time we traveled to or from any of our stations we had to pay all our expenses. There was no assistance from the mission to help with the cost to reach to or from our stations. With the small salary that my husband received it was getting more and more costly to visit home. Traveling the distance from the extreme north of the country to the last town south with all our children was also very inconvenient.

One day, after seeing that I was looking so sad, Mr. Justo Villas invited me to go with a few his friends and members of his family on a sailing trip around the lagoon. Mr. Villas, one of the well-to-do men of the village, was a good friend of our family. I gladly accepted the invitation. This was during the school holiday so my husband agreed to stay home with the children.

We sailed far out in the sailboat but within a short time just as I was enjoying the trip we began to return. Mr. Villas must have noticed the look on my face and figured out what I was thinking because he asked me, "Would you like to sail some more?"

"Yes, surely please," I gladly answered.

We sailed to and fro, and around and around the lagoon. I enjoyed the scenery, and the sunny, windy, and beautiful weather. The sky was clear and blue and the surroundings looked so bright and green. The boat ride felt very relaxing. I felt as if I were far away from everything. For those few hours, I didn't have to worry about anything. As we all just sat in the boat we shared jokes and laughed a lot and everyone felt so happy. The sailing was such a rare break from all that I had gotten used to doing.

When I got back home I felt new. The sad feeling that was bearing me down for the past few weeks had gone away. After that trip I no longer had the sad feeling and the longing I had for returning home to Punta Gorda seemed to have disappeared. I felt so light-hearted that I did not mind patiently waiting until we could afford a family trip to Punta Gorda. I am always thankful to Mr. Villas for that trip.

In the month of December 1928, after almost three years away, our family was finally able to return home to Punta Gorda to spend the Christmas holidays. There was only one little problem that happened just before we left but Mr. Enriquez made sure that this was not going to hold us back. There was no direct passage available from Progresso to Corozal Town so he had to hire a dory to take us there in time to catch the boat to Belize. The owner of the dory along with Mr. Enriquez and I had to paddle all the way down to Los Cocos Lagoon then to Corozal where we took the boat, Romulus, to Belize City. From there we caught the other boat to Punta Gorda where we spent the Christmas holidays with our people.

As always, everyone at home was very glad to see us and we were also very happy to reunite with them. Christmas was usually one big family celebration time that we enjoyed with my mother, my sisters, my husband's relatives and their family. This was a time for our children to also spend some time with their cousins, aunts, uncles and other relatives.

During this season I also enjoyed visiting the homes of family and friends in Punta Gorda, or receive visitors, and also watch the popular native John Canoe dances that were performed all around the town by the Garifuna men. The Christmas season was also a time when we got visits from relatives and friends who live in Livingston, Puerto Barrios or Bananera in Guatemala. Many Garifuna families in Punta Gorda have relatives who lived or worked in those places. When they visit Punta Gorda during Christmas, they added fun to the celebrations with the different stories they shared from all the places that they came from. The Christmas season was also the time when many teachers returned home with their families after several months at their different stations. It was a happy time to catch up with family and friends, and meet new visitors.

## *Farewell to Progresso Village*

During the course of our Christmas holidays in Punta Gorda, Fr. Tenk told Mr. Enriquez that he would be very grateful if he would go back to take over the San Antonio school again if possible. Fr. Tenk explained that a group of Maya leaders had met with him and explained that if Mr. Enriquez could not go back to them, they would prefer to have the school closed as they did not like the other teachers who had succeeded him. The school was going through a lot of problems and there were a number of changes in teachers. None of them wanted to stay in the village for a long time. Mr. Enriquez asked me my opinion about the matter, but it was not easy for me to decide especially when I remembered the difficulties we had traveling with the small children.

Around this time we were only renting a house. Ours, including the fence and the rest of the property, was in a rundown condition. A few months earlier while we were in Progresso, our family in Punta Gorda had sent us a letter advising my husband to return home and start to build a convenient dwelling house for himself and his family, as sickness and death would surely come sometime or another. They said that if our Lord called one of us at any time it would be very difficult for the family, since we would not be prepared. During the Christmas holiday visit, the elders of our family also reminded us about the advice they had written in the letter. This advice had penetrated his mind so deeply that he decided we would return home after a year or so as soon as the management decides.

After being away from home for so long, we also realized that the Christmas break was too short for us to look after our property and take care of other family business. Moreover, I wanted to spend more time with my family. They also insisted that the children and I spend more time with them. We all decided that instead of spending all that money for traveling back and then spending again to return a few months later for the long May vacation, the children and I would remain home in Punta Gorda for a few more months while Mr. Enriquez returned alone to Progresso to complete the school year. He would return to Punta Gorda for the May vacation, after which we would all return to Progresso for another year or two before returning home for good. That was our plan.

Spending that extra time with my family was one of the best decisions that we made. With the support of my mother, sisters and relatives I was able to rest more. Some days I didn't even have to do household duties as my sisters shared food and offered to clean the house. On Sundays my mother, sisters and I shared the cooking for each other and enjoyed the afternoon sharing stories about our life. This was the first time since my marriage that I had spent so much time with them and away from my husband. The children also enjoyed all the special attention and love that they were getting from so many family members. Even though the people of Progresso liked them, it felt so different to see them get all the attention from so many extended family members for a long time. Those extra months with family in Punta Gorda were very good for all of us.

When Mr. Enriquez returned from Progresso at the end of May, I was surprised to see that he brought back all our belongings. He had decided that he would accept the offer to return to San Antonio so as to be closer to home. We would no longer return to Progresso. He told me that the people of Progresso gave him a grand farewell party and that he was not even given a chance to pack up our belongings or carry them; the people did everything for him. He showed me all the gifts that they sent me which included a cut of dress cloth, cups and saucers, some pretty table glasses, table napkins, pillows cases and more than a dozen photos of families and friends. He reported that the people of the village all cried when he left.

That day I wept a lot as I thought about my life with the people of Progresso and especially when I realized that I did not get a chance to embrace and say my final good-byes to any of them. When we left the village, it was only for the Christmas vacation. It was never our intention to remain in Punta Gorda. I had never thought that I would never see them again. I never realized that I had felt so much a part of the people there and that I had gotten to like them very much. Maybe Progresso was a very special place for me because three of my children were born there. All my memories of the kindness of the people also made Progresso very special to me.

A few days later, I sent a letter to the people to say goodbye and to thank them for all the kindness that they showed me during our long stay there. I also thanked them for the wonderful gifts they sent me and told them that it is my wish that the shower of God's blessing descend upon them.

## *Barranco*

Instead of going to work in San Antonio in the month of June 1929, the school manager sent us to the Garifuna village of Barranco, twelve miles by sea south of Punta Gorda. The rainy season had

Barranco village gathering after Mass. Photo by Fr. Fusz (served Punta Gorda 1908-1914).

Students, Parents, and Teachers in front of St. Joseph Church in Barranco, early 1940s, before the 1945 hurricane.

made the trail to San Antonio very difficult for us to travel with our very young children.

My husband took over the Barranco school from Alejandro Ogaldez, who had been holding over from January to May that year as a replacement for Henry Loredo, a native of Barranco.

It was at Barranco that our other baby boy, Equitius, was born to us on August 11, 1929.

The living conditions of our family in Barranco were horrible and far different than what we had been used to in Progresso and El Cayo. The house in which we stayed was rundown and in need of much repair. Although it had a verandah all around, its walls had about one inch open spaces in between each lumber on all sides, and its gable was half open. The constant draught that flowed inside this house was what caused me to become ill with another severe attack of neuralgia shortly after we settled there. My face became so twisted that I had to be rushed to the doctor in Punta Gorda for treatment.

The house also attracted many bats and at nights we all had to sleep under a net to prevent them from sucking us. However, the nets did not always keep the bats out. Many mornings I noticed that when the children woke up, their feet or fingers would be bleeding from the bites of these pests. Within a few weeks we found a sure way to get rid of them. We soaked some cotton balls with carbo negus and hung them at various sections the beam. Because of the stench of this disinfectant, the bats departed for good and we became safe.

Despite these difficulties, I felt quite happy to be at home among our people as we tried as best as we could to adjust to our living conditions. Unlike the other places where we were stationed, Barranco was the place where some of my relatives lived. For example, the Palacios, who are my cousins, all come from Basilia Arana nee Labriel, who is the sister of my grandmother Petrona Zuniga nee Labriel.

It was in Barranco that we spoke our Garifuna language most, not only at home but with everyone in the community. Because we didn't speak Garifuna outside our home in San Antonio, or El Cayo, or Progresso or any other community where we were stationed, speaking our language everywhere, and being with relatives made us feel very much at home. It was so good to see our older children getting better at speaking their Garifuna language with their new friends. Besides speaking Spanish and English very well, they became much better at speaking Garifuna during the year that we stayed in Barranco.

Mr. Enriquez was quite surprised that the Barranco school was not up to standard as it should be. This demanded more of his time and efforts. He found that many of the school children were not up to standard in basic skills and discipline. The school records also showed that for about six years, from 1923 to 1929, before Mr. Enriquez arrived in Barranco, there was a decline in the number of students passing the school examinations. Because of this, he spent a lot of extra time with the pupils to correct most of their weaknesses. He had to be very firm to make sure that the students improved on discipline, personal hygiene and personal appearance in school. He gave them extra home lessons and a lot of advice about the importance of school to their future. He also had meetings with the parents to ask for their cooperation. By the end of our stay, he was pleased that the pupils were showing much improvement in their schoolwork and exams. The parents were very pleased at the progress that was made in a short time.

It is my understanding that the other time when the school at Barranco did very well in their exams was during the period between 1917 and 1922 when Simeon Sampson was in charge. After Mr. Sampson, Mr. Henry Loredo from Barranco took charge of the school from January 1923 to November 1928. After Mr. Loredo left, Mr. Alejandro Ogaldez became the head teacher for a few months, from January to May 1929, before my husband took charge in June that year. After we left Barranco in August 1930, Mr. Santos Arzu took charge of the school there for about two years before it was taken over by Mr. Salvatore Daniels for a number of years.

## *TOPCO*

From Barranco, we were transferred to TOPCO (Tropical Oil Products Company) where we would remain for about fifteen months from September 1930 to December 1931. The plans for our transfer to San Antonio was put on hold as we tried as much as possible to be nearer to our family in Punta Gorda, especially with the newborn child and the other young children.

TOPCO was the name of an American German company. This big operation with its community of workers and their families was located upstream of the Rio Grande, the river just north of Punta Gorda. The company gathered cohune nuts from trees that grew abundantly in the area and processed these into cohune oil and gun powder. These products were sent on barges down the river and far out at sea where ships waited to be loaded. From there the ships transported these products to foreign countries.

Unlike other communities where we served, TOPCO was quite a mix of different ethnic groups who came there to find work in the cohune operations. There were East Indians, Mestizos, Creole, Maya, English and American people living there. Others came from Honduras and Guatemala. Many Garifuna people were employed there as laborers and supervisors. During that time Mr. Enriquez's cousin Ambrocio Noralez, who was the youngest son of his Aunt Juliana Noralez nee Colindres and his uncle Martin Noralez (Yau Sasu), worked as the chief commissar at the company's commissary.

At first Mr. Enriquez was worried about our transfer from Barranco to TOPCO. The more he thought about it, the more he realized that the additional expenses of traveling and living there would be very costly for us. This move would only add to the numerous debts that we had already incurred. However, as was the practice, we had to go wherever the priest decided to send us even though the entire cost of moving came from my husband's pocket. This was how it was when teachers were transferred; they paid for everything. Even before this transfer, Mr. Enriquez had already spent more than his salary could repay due to the fact that after we returned from Progresso, our house was in such a run-down condition that we had to rent another house in Punta Gorda before we proceeded to Barranco. Furthermore, the previous illnesses of the family, the doctor's treatment, the travels to and from our station, and other expenses all increased our debt.

To reach TOPCO we had to walk to Westmoreland, about six miles from Punta Gorda not far from the East Indian village called Elridge, then through another road to the bank of the river and cross over by boat. Another way to get there was by boat from Punta Gorda up the Rio Grande; the community was on the right bank a few miles up the Rio Grande.

As it turned out, TOPCO was a great blessing and relief for us. Had it not been for our transfer there, we wouldn't have been able to repay our debts. There I took up sewing and baking, and everything I made was always sold out, no matter how much I made. The sales that I made to the company manager, the workers and their families turned out so well that I was able to cover almost all of our family food and other home expenses while my husband's salary went towards paying off our debts. It was at TOPCO that I made the most amount of money I had ever made for my family.

Mr. Enriquez and I also got along very well with Mr. Oliver Kisseck, the Manager of the operation, his wife Mrs. Kisseck, and the people. After seeing the poor condition of the small house that our family was crowded in, Mr. Kisseck promised to provide us better housing. He also raised my husband's salary since the school was not government aided at the time. The arrangement was that the mission would pay half of my husband's salary through the kindness of the late Fr. Allan Stevenson, pastor and manager of the Catholic mission, and the company would pay the other half. The total salary was forty dollars a month. These arrangements eventually made our living condition much better than we had expected.

Since our family did not yet own a good house, Mr. Enriquez decided to have one built in Punta Gorda. After he finished paying his debt, he saved some of his earnings while I managed the home with whatever I earned from my sewing and baking. That was the way we built the house that we have now.

During the month of May 1931, I became very ill with diarrhea and vomiting. By then we were to have gone home to Punta Gorda for the holidays but we delayed because Mr. Enriquez was in charge of taking the census in the village that month. Apart from me, almost all the rest of the children—Olivia, Elicia, Solomon and Equitius—also became ill. I was so ill that I was not able to take good care of my sick little baby boy, Equitius. Of the entire family, only Mr. Enriquez and our two-year-old Peter were well. I will always be thankful for kindness shown by Mr. and Mrs. Kisseck during the illnesses of our family members. They visited often and whatever we needed, they gave us freely. They both made extra effort to ensure that we were comfortable. They gave us a variety of delicious foods such as oats, cream custard, peaches and grapes but because of our illness none of us could have eaten anything.

Sadly for us, our baby Equitius did not survive the illness. He died three months short of his second birthday. Although I was not among my people when this happened, I did not feel any loneliness. The people of TOPCO were so kind and helpful and we got all the necessary help from them. Mrs. Kisseck brought a ribbon and medal for the deceased baby. Mr. Flowers of the Salvation Army Schools in the district offered to dig the grave. Mr. Tenasoff built the coffin and a Spanish lady, whose name I now forget, offered to make the shawl. Another Spanish lady made a wreath and bouquet of artificial roses. All of this help was in addition to those who consoled us and kept us company at the wake that night.

When the time came for the funeral the next day, there was a heavy downpour of rain. Despite this, Mrs. Kisseck came running through the showers to be at home with me before the baby's body was placed in the coffin. There was a big crowd at home. Everyone prayed and sang hymns over the deceased. We thanked them for that.

Seeing my affliction when the body was put in the coffin, Mrs. Kisseck opened her arms wide and I instantly threw myself there as I wept. The first stroke of the hammer as the men sealed the coffin, felt like another blow to my heart. This time, I could not contain myself; I wept loudly.

Mrs. Kisseck embraced me tightly as she calmly repeated, "Mrs. Enriquez, always remember that God giveth and God taketh back."

Although it is natural for a mother to weep over the loss of a child, I tried my best to control myself up from all my weeping. However, it took a while to regain control of myself.

Mrs. Kisseck didn't go to the funeral. Instead she stayed with me at home to comfort me. For some hours after, she looked after the surviving children, who were still very sick, and took some time to comfort them especially after they had seen the lifeless body of their little brother.

Two days after the funeral, Mr. Enriquez and I walked down to the landing, now known as "Cattle Landing," with the sick children. We didn't get to travel in any of the company vehicles as was planned because all vehicles were being used that week for the cohune operations. We couldn't wait longer because Mr. Enriquez was also going to take his teacher's exam. Instead we were offered only two mules to carry our luggage. All through the miles that we walked, Mr. Enriquez carried seven-year-old Elicia on his back while I carried four-year-old Peter, for although he wasn't sick, he was too young to walk such a long distance. The older children, Olivia being the oldest at eleven years, Zenobia nine years, and Solomon six years, also had to walk the entire journey even though they were not in good health. I was also in the early stage of pregnancy.

As we walked along the way, the bright weather suddenly began to change. Dark clouds were covering the sky. If it rained, we would surely become soaking wet, which could cause the very sick children to surely get pneumonia. We were very worried about this. When Mr. Enriquez saw the dark clouds were getting thicker, he asked us to stop walking. He knelt down on the road, closed his eyes and prayed deeply, stretching forth his hand heavenwards to the heavy black clouds and made the sign of the cross. Gradually, the threatening stormy weather vanished. We got to the landing safely and were very thankful for this.

Unfortunately at the landing, the only boat was already full and could not take all of us. I had to stay there with the sick children while my husband proceeded alone by boat to Punta Gorda for the teachers' exam. He remained in Punta Gorda for two days and two nights searching for passage for us, and worrying because the children did not have the appetite to eat anything. At long last, we traveled from the landing to Punta Gorda in a motorboat and arrived there feeling and looking all worn out and ill.

Immediately Mr. Enriquez and I took the children to the hospital. Since there was no car we had to carry each of them on our backs. Dr. Savonnah said that Olivia had influenza; Elicia was homesick and was in need of sea air. Along with the influenza, Solomon also had hookworms. None of the children could be admitted to the hospital because there were no beds available. There were many who were also ill at that time and all the beds were occupied. That kind and blessed doctor made it his duty to walk from the hospital to my mother's house near the cemetery to take good care of these children for me. When he could not visit, he sent the nurse. We were so grateful. May God bless his soul!

One evening as the sick children slept, I sat alone in the bedroom for a while thinking about all that my family had been through over the years but especially recently. I thought about the hard work and sacrifices that my husband has done for so many people. Ever since we were married we were always traveling and working amongst other people, many times under harsh conditions. It was getting harder to travel with our young children. I thought about all the illnesses that our family had been through because of difficult living conditions that we had to get used to. That evening, I cried again remembering the recent death of baby Equitius, the illness that permanently affected Elicia, the illnesses that my husband, children and I had been through. I remembered how sad it was when I lost my first five children who were stillborn because of the hard conditions of life in San Antonio. I remembered the hours of walking barefooted along with my husband through the forest and hills to and from the village, even while pregnant. As I watched my poor sick children, I thought about how they also had to get used to traveling and living in different places and conditions.

At the same time I also remembered the many friendly, kind and good people that we met and became good friends with as we worked in their community. I wondered when the time would come for us to settle in one place in our own house as a family. For a long time that evening, about two weeks before I turned 37 years old, I sat alone thinking about all these things. I was also expecting another child in a few months. It was our prayers that gave me much strength to bear all this. I believed more that whatever happened, whatever is happening and whatever will happen is all in the hands of the Almighty and I leave it all up to Him.

When the fever left my children, the doctor told me, "Now, Mrs. Enriquez, cover them up; lest draught, pneumonia and death."

I tried my best to follow his advice. Since we didn't yet have any house of our own, I had to keep them at my sister's upstairs house. Oh you should have seen Olivia and especially Solomon; they looked so weak and thin that you could have counted their bones. If we had stayed at TOPCO, Solomon surely would have died. Because he was so sick and skinny, his father didn't even have the heart to look at him.

Eventually, the doctor had to give the boy an injection to strengthen him. As a result of the injection, however, his seat had become so swollen that he was unable to sit. I had to remain at his bedside to help him turn.

One day, while Solomon and I were waiting at the clinic to see the doctor, a lady who was visiting the hospital saw that the swollen condition of my son and asked, "What is the matter with your little boy?"

"The injection that he got from the doctor caused the swelling," I told her.

The lady who looked more frightened than me said, "You know that is dangerous? I had seen something happen like that once. There was a certain man who got his seat swollen after the injection. You know, he died!"

Although I was tired and sleepy, after staying up almost all night looking after my son, I tried to be patient as I listened to her complaining badly about the hospital. She continued with one negative story after another to try to discourage me from continuing the treatment with the doctor and the hospital.

When she finished complaining, I answered, "I am 36 years old, soon to be 37. I had five stillborn children before, and God gave me the five I now have. He also took away a baby son from me recently. He giveth, He taketh. So if it is His will to remove all my children from me, one after another, I will bear my cross and tighten my waist like a woman to bear it all."

From that time, nobody could tell me anything to make me worry or feel discouraged. I just listened to my good doctor and kind nurses. The doctor, my mother, my sisters and I, were all very glad to see the children recovering their health. The doctor told me that as soon as Solomon gained enough strength to walk a little, I must carry him to the hospital for hookworm treatment.

The first day that I took Solomon to the hospital I found that he could not walk there all the way; he was so weak that he got tired easily. Along the way to the hospital, we had to sit several times at different shops to rest. After his first treatment that day, the doctor told me not to give him anything to eat and not until two o'clock in the afternoon to give him a cup of milk.

My mother noticed that I didn't care to give Solomon anything to eat and with a very worried look she asked me, "Are you not going to give this child something to eat or drink? He is so weak to stay so long without anything in his stomach."

"Don't worry, Mama," I replied, "the doctor said that he would not feel hungry." My mother was so sorry for him.

After his third treatment, Solomon felt much better.

At the end of June 1931, sadness came upon the family again when Mr. Enriquez's first cousin Ambrocio Noralez took away his own life at the tender age of 19 years. As I mentioned before, Ambrocio was the youngest son of Mr. Enriquez's aunt Juliana Colindres, also known as Da Blackie. She was the aunt who raised Mr. Enriquez and served as his mother when her sister, Mr. Enriquez's mother, passed away while he was still a boy. Ambrocio had been doing so well as the commisar at the company's commisary in TOPCO that no one suspected this sudden death. It was especially painful for his mother.

I was never able to return with my husband for the reopening of the school until August since all this time the children were taking treatment.

Everybody returned to perfect health by the time we went back to TOPCO in late August. Once there, I continued with my baking and sewing in order to finish paying the doctor's bill and other bills. Some of people whom we owed were sympathetic with us and were willing to wait until we could gradually pay the balance. The doctor did not charge us much.

Around this time also, our house in Punta Gorda was being built. The company's manager was so willing to help us that my husband bought all the lumber through him. First, my husband ordered some local bush building materials such as thatch leaves, sticks and tie-ties. These materials were later lost because we had no proper place to store them. We had stored these materials under a neighbour's house but we lost them while she was away and we had to buy another set of materials.

Finally my husband gave some money to a carpenter and made arrangements for construction to begin. He promised to pay the carpenter every month; not every fortnight as the carpenter had wanted. The agreement was settled and the carpenter began building. A few weeks later however, the carpenter started to ask for money every two weeks. My husband got annoyed and told carpenter to stop working. Friends, neighbours and family members noticed and agreed that the work was poorly done so my husband had to hire another carpenter.

The situation was even worse than we thought when the new carpenter complained that the work of the first carpenter was so badly done that he could not finish it that way.

"Moreover," the new carpenter said, "I don't want people to say that it was I who did such a bad work in building your house."

My husband agreed with the new carpenter's request to tear the work down and start building all over again. The carpenter tore down everything, rooted out the posts, dug fresh holes for the foundation and started from scratch. All the money that had been paid to the former carpenter had gone to nothing. I managed to get back some of the sticks and leaves that were stolen.

On December 5th, when I woke up in the morning, I had a slight pain. When I told my husband about it he answered, "What are we going to do and how are we going to manage? You are a woman who never last long with pain. Moreover the nurse is not here in the settlement. I understand that she went down to Punta Gorda yesterday."

Also worried about the situation I replied, "Can you go and ask Mr. Turner or Mr. Luis for a boat to take me to Punta Gorda?"

When my husband returned, he explained that he had met a few men who were willing to paddle a dory with me directly down to Punta Gorda. However, I did not accept this offer. Because of the long distance, I would not arrive home on time and my pains would only get worse along the way.

I went myself to ask Mr. Turner again to send the motorboat with me. I explained that I was having birth pains and the nurse was not there to assist. Mr. Turner offered me a free trip as long as we furnished the gasoline. We then walked down through the bush to the landing pier and to the motorboat that took us Perret's landing—owned by the mahogany contractor, Mr. Sidney Perret. From there we had to walk a good distance through a rough pasture, before catching a car to Punta Gorda.

Interior of the old Peter Claver Church in Punta Gorda in the 1940s.

School children in front of the Peter Claver Parish Hall and Pallotine Convent in Punta Gorda awaiting a visit of Bishop Murphy in the 1930s

It seemed as though the smooth motorboat ride did me a great deal of good because I felt much better as soon as we arrived home safely to my mother that same Saturday. All day Sunday I was feeling better and my husband returned to the village to be there for the last week of school. Late that same Sunday night, December 7, 1931, bringing in Monday, Constantine Gregory Enriquez was born at my mother's house.

In the early days of January 1932, we moved into our new house. This accomplishment made me feel as if I were in a dream. After all the trials and troubles with expenses before, we finally got to live in a house of our own. I was so happy that sometimes I couldn't even sleep wondering if my eyes were deceiving me. For the kitchen, my husband built a temporary hut until a few years later when he built a decent one.

## *Crique Sarco*

When school reopened in January of that year, Mr. Enriquez was transferred to Crique Sarco. He had asked me not to go with him on this trip because he would only be there for only a few months. Moreover, the baby was too young to travel and our four-year-old Peter was sick. Upon hearing this, I quietly agreed because I knew that he had already gotten an appointment to return to San Antonio in June.

Unfortunately, shortly after my husband settled in the village, he found himself quite lonely. Since the place was very far out of the way, he could not visit nor hear from us as often as he would like. This inconvenience made him decide to return for our family around the end of that month. With very short notice, I willingly got ready to go. I was missing him too.

On the day of our departure, I got up at 3:00 o'clock in the morning, woke up the children, combed them, and got them dressed before I dressed myself. Because I had only recently given birth to a baby, I made sure to keep my body warm for the journey. To protect my body from draught of the cold west wind that was blowing strongly that morning, I wore a warm outfit with long sleeves. I also wore stockings, shoes, and a head tie or kerchief shawl to keep my head warm. Around my waist I tied a bandage to support my back for the long hours of sitting in the dory. I also checked again to make sure that all the children were dressed warmly.

The day before, I had packed up most of our provisions, clothing and utensils that we would need for our stay in the village. That morning Mr. Enriquez completed the final packing and the Punta Gorda men we had hired came to carry our luggage to the boat. Lastly, I wrapped my little baby with a blanket, closed the door and we all marched down to the seashore that cool dark morning.

As soon as we reached the shore, the men loaded our luggage in the dory and prepared it for travel. After the dory was neatly packed, the children got in and found their seats, just before the men pushed the bow out to sea. Only the front end of the dory was touching the shore for the rest of us to get in without getting our feet wet. As the children waited, the adults loaded the final smaller pieces of luggage. Just as we were about to get in, however, we noticed that a lot of water had leaked into the boat through a big hole at the bottom. This caused the children to get their warm covered feet soaking wet. The men pulled the dory back to shore, took out all the children, unloaded some of the luggage and patched the leak.

I felt so badly about what was happening that early morning that I said to myself, "You children are supposed to be in your beds snuggly and warm instead of getting wet in the early cold morning. Look what happened after all I did to make sure that you were kept warm."

Patching the leak did not take a long time. While the men were reloading the dory, I felt the need to use the toilet before the long trip. Since my eldest daughter Olivia was still on shore, I gave her the baby to hold and then walked on the pier towards the latrine. The morning was still dark. Being unfamiliar with the pier, I thought that it was built as one piece with a latrine on each side of the end as I had usually seen in other parts of Punta Gorda. My mind was convinced that the entire length of the pier to the latrine over the sea was one piece so I walked with full confidence towards its shadowy outline that dark morning. I did not realize that the pier had a scissors-like split about half way, with each section leading to a separate latrine. Since none of the other latrines was built in that way, it didn't cross my mind that this one was different.

Alas! With one big splash, I fell into the sea. I felt a sharp pain on my face and my legs as I hit the side of the pier as I fell. My clothes and my entire body got soaking wet.

Immediately I heard my husband calling out, "You fell down?"

"Yes," I shouted fearfully below the pier as I tried to stand on the rocky bottom of the sea that was about shoulder deep.

Over the sound of the light waves, I heard my husband shouting for help. Both he and my uncle who was one of our traveling companions rushed to help. At that time, I was in good health and weighed some pounds. Each held one of my arms and pulled me up to the pier. You could have heard the sound of a heavy shower pouring out from my body as I stood on the pier.

When I got ashore, I was shivering and crying with cold and fright. I felt the bruises and scratches on my face. Later in the early morning light, I saw my legs were also blue with bruises. In the dark, under a tree near the shore I tried to look for my clothes among the luggage but couldn't find any. In packing all my belongings, I had never expected such a thing to happen. Moreover we had no flashlight and no lanterns to search for what I wanted from the luggage. Feeling around inside the luggage I managed to find one single thin nightgown to put on my bare body. No longer did I have the underwear, or bandage, or shoes or stockings that I had carefully worn to make sure that I kept warm. I had to take all those off and wear the thin nightgown until there was enough early morning light to find my other clothes. The strong, cold morning breeze on my soaking wet body made me shiver. The bad cold I caught after this incident caused me to be unable to bear any more children.

The leaky boat, our wet children and my fall were all a rough start for the day's journey. My husband kept saying how sorry he was about all this and wondered if it was a good idea to have come for his family after all.

By the time the early morning light broke in the horizon we were on our way out at sea. We were passing my mother's landing in the southern part of Punta Gorda, when I saw my uncle's wife standing at the seashore. I asked the men to stop on shore for a short while so that I could explain to her all that had happened. I asked her to tell my mother that I had gotten badly hurt from falling into the sea from the latrine wharf but that I would be alright.

As we traveled along, I felt so sad that tears silently rolled down my cheeks. Whenever I looked at my children quietly sitting together beside me and in the dory seat in front of me, I couldn't help but look out at sea as I kept wiping the tears. The bruises on my body were painful but my tears were more for the sympathy I felt for our children traveling again to another remote place after all that they had already been through. We hardly got a chance to live in our new house. Travelling with family to live from one place to another for my husband's teaching job, were hard sacrifices that our family had made that many people scarcely know about or even imagine. My husband often explained that through these sacrifices we were following God's will to educate people and lead them out of a life of darkness to make them good solid Christians for themselves and for their future generations. As he dedicated himself to his work and family, I also wanted to fulfill my duty as his wife to make sure that he was always well taken care of.

From Punta Gorda we traveled all day along the coast as the men paddled our dory past the mouth of the Moho River and Barranco, and then up the Temash River further south. By the time we arrived at Camp Ke along the Temash River, it was late in the evening. There we managed to find an old abandoned building to spend the night. This shack that was almost covered with overgrown bush had no walls; only the roof and mud flooring. We decided that there was no choice but to find shelter there. My husband, uncle, and the other men had to chop and clean out the very high bush from around the entire building. There was where we spent the night with the baby and our other children. That dark night, while everyone was asleep I listened to the sounds of the forest and also heard one of the men snoring as I thought about all that had happened during the long day of travel. I felt very tired from a very long day but I was the last to fall asleep. Because of their hard physical work of paddling the dory and clearing out the bush, the men were the first to fall asleep shortly after the children. Alone, I prayed for health and strength for our family in the new village that we were going to live in. Then I fell sound asleep.

The next day, we awoke very early, ate a quick breakfast from the food we had packed for the trip, and continued up the river with the men paddling the whole journey upstream the Temash River to Crique Sarco.

As soon as we arrived in the village, we walked straight to the teacher's house. Mr. Enriquez wanted to make sure that we were settled in first, before he introduced us to the people.

The main teacher's house was in a horrible condition. Some sections of the wall were covered with a green and black moldy matter that was caused by continuous dampness. Other sections were still wet from rains some days before. The entire house needed a thorough cleaning and that's what my husband, the older children and I immediately did. It was a good thing that it was not during the rainy season that we had to stay in those houses. Besides, there were some low lying areas near the house that could hold big pools of water in the rainy season and cause malaria. Under such living arrangements we were lucky to be there for only a few months.

At Crique Sarco I managed to bake bread for sale. I also made almost one sack of starch for sale in Punta Gorda in order to help buy food and other needs for the children. The sales I made at Crique Sarco, however, were not even close to what I had made during our time at TOPCO. This time my husband's salary was only $30.00 per month, down from $40.00 per month he had earned at TOPCO. With my reduced earnings from sales and with my husband's big drop in salary, it was a little more difficult for us to meet our expenses. We returned home to Punta Gorda at the end of the school term and spent our vacation there up to the end of May 1932.

## *Return to San Antonio Village, Toledo District*

It was at the beginning of the month of June 1932 that we learned that the Mayas from San Antonio had presented another petition to the Manager of Catholic schools, Rev, Herman J. Tenk, S.J., for the return of my husband to teach in San Antonio. This time it was a written petition signed by several more villagers. The petition stated again that without Mr. Enriquez the villagers would rather have the school closed.

The Manager discussed the matter with my husband, then handed him the petition. My husband in turn showed the petition to me when he arrived home. Although we had talked about this move some months before, I again pointed out the difficulty of going to such a distant outpost with our young children. It would have been better for the School Manager to consider having us work in our hometown or as near as possible. I argued that all our life we had been moving around to several different places; all the strain of travelling and settling into a new place and moving again to another was a big sacrifice for our family, especially the children. We should not have to continue to live like this.

Moreover, we were the ones who always had to bear the expenses of moving. I also argued that our children were too young to walk such a long distance from Punta Gorda to San Antonio. Besides, there was also the essential luggage to take along for our young children and myself. After my argument, Mr. Enriquez explained that he had already discussed these concerns and the priest had promised that we would remain in the village for a longer time. We would not have to worry about moving to another place again within a short time. He convinced me that the manager also made an agreement with the Mayas to transport our luggage from Punta Gorda to San Antonio. Then he explained that because the School Manager was puzzled about how to answer the petition, and because of the promises the school manager made, he would accept the job.

Fr. Tenk was so glad when my husband informed him of his acceptance. Fr. Tenk immediately notified the villagers to be ready to come for us for the re-opening of school. We were told that when the villagers got the news, they all rejoiced.

A few days before the re-opening of school, about ten Maya men arrived with seven horses to fetch my husband and I and our six children. We packed our bundles, sorting out which luggage to take along first since the horses could not take all that we wanted. Since the road to San Antonio was not yet built, much of the traveling around that time was done on horseback through trails in the forest. The building of the Punta Gorda-San Antonio Road had only begun in 1935 and it was not completed until the early 1940s.

Very early the following morning, just before daybreak, we set out on our journey. Each horse was loaded with luggage. Each of the Maya men, my husband, and the older children also carried whatever piece of luggage that they could. Within the first few miles, my arms got very tired from holding the baby, Constantine. Mr. Enriquez could not help me because he was also carrying some luggage. Seeing this, the Maya men taught me how to sling the baby on my back with the use of a sheet tied with *mecapal*, which are strips of tree bark that they used for tying their bundles. This Maya way of carrying my baby provided rest for my arms as I walked. The older children, Olivia and Zenobia, walked the entire journey while the younger ones—Elicia, Solomon and Peter—took turns riding on the horse. Walking beside each horse was a Maya man to hold the rope and guide it along the way.

Our first rest stop was about two hours later at Jacinto Creek. There we had breakfast, since we had left Punta Gorda too early to eat. Moreover we were unable to drink at least some hot tea before we started our journey that morning because we were very busy with our final packing for the trip. Usually we would start our journey on an empty stomach because we always wanted to start very early in the morning to take advantage of the cool weather and to arrive at our last stop for the day just before sundown.

After Jacinto Creek, the next rest stop for lunch was at Crique Piedra. From there we travelled to Murphy Die and finally to San Antonio.

The villagers were on the look out at the highest hill in the village, and could see us from a distance as we approached. There on top of the hill, which is now called Burns Hill, they kept watchful sight. As we got nearer, we saw them running to and fro pointing to our direction to inform the others that we were in sight. When we got to the top of the hill, we noticed that there wasn't a house near that area from which someone did not peep out.

The whole community came out to greet us at the village entrance. When we arrived at the teacher's quarters, almost everybody brought us some cacao drinks and tortillas without meat. As was their customary greeting, they asked us about our health and asked if we were still alive.

It was the custom of the Mayas that when they meet a person whom they had not seen for a long time they would ask as a form of greeting, "So you are still living?" or "So you are not dead yet?"

Some of our old friends cried for joy to see us return to their native village once more. It was about fourteen years since we were last there. When we asked about the other friends we had from our first stay we learned that a number of them had passed away. All remembered that I had nursed their babies when they were only months old. I noticed that the village had grown bigger than it was when we were first stationed there.

The people were also surprised to see that our six children were all healthy and strong. It was the first time that they were seeing our children since they were all born after we left San Antonio in April 1918. Our eldest child Olivia was almost 14 years old and she was going to assist as a pupil teacher at the school. The youngest was the baby, Constantine, who was only six months old. As we settled in, we received visitors at our home every day. Many visited to share news about what had happened in the village over the years that we were not there. Others, brought yams, eggs, coco, plantains, and whatever they wanted to share.

Because of the shortage of horses, we had to leave some of our essential household needs at home in Punta Gorda. The men who had assisted us, refused to return for the remainder of our belongings as they had promised. Without the washbowl, tub and scrub board, I had to wash clothes in the river. This sickened me with a strong head and chest cold, and a hoarseness that I could have barely heard what I was saying. For an entire week, I was so hoarse that I could only use hand signals to communicate with others. We had to wait until the end of the month to send for the remainder of our belongings.

Within a short time our children all settled in well. They quickly made new friends and learned another new language. By this time the older ones spoke Garifuna, English, and Spanish very well. They picked up the Maya language quite quickly from their new Maya friends. My husband and I also practiced speaking Maya with the children at home. It was interesting how as a family we could communicate amongst ourselves in one language or another. At home we spoke mainly Garifuna and English but when we were with friends or visitors from the community we spoke Maya. It was good to see all our children talking Maya to their new friends as they played or worked together. Those villagers who could speak Spanish were also surprised when they heard our older children speaking that language.

A few months after we settled in at San Antonio, we received the sad news about the sudden death of Mr. Enriquez's aunt Juliana Noralez nee Colindres, who was also known as Da Blackie. She was only 53 years old when she died on March 25, 1933. It was Da Blackie who had raised Mr. Enriquez, his only brother Sylverius, and his only sister Rosenda after their parents died. Mr. Enriquez, the eldest child of his parents, was about twelve years old when his parents died. Da Blackie was the younger sister of his late mother, Maria Genera Enriquez nee Colindres.

## *My Call to Healing*

I realized soon that my return to San Antonio must have been to become better in my new interest in healing. All of my life's experiences in the past must have been to prepare me for this. After the family illnesses that my family and I had been through over the years, I had decided to learn from my elder relatives some of the traditional remedies that they used to keep them well and to heal whatever illnesses they had. Because I had lived most of the time outside of my hometown, I had not taken the chance to learn this, and was not too interested then. During the months that we returned from Progresso, and especially after all the illnesses that my children got, I decided to make a serious effort to learn all I could to protect and heal my family. But I did not think I would be helping others.

This started in a strange way. One morning in July, the month after we arrived in San Antonio, a woman came to me asking if it would be possible for me to help her with a health situation. She said she had a belief that my soul would, in the name of our good Creator, cure her.

"But why did you come to me thinking that I could heal you?" I asked.

"My mind told me to come to you. I know that you can heal me!" she pleaded. "You have strong healthy children, you must know something. I only have one child with my second husband. Moreover, my mother-in-law sent me to you and my husband, the teacher's god-son, said that whatever it costs, he will pay you if you could attend to me."

Mr. Enriquez also had many godsons in the village. Whenever people reminded me about their son or relative being my husband's godson, it always meant that they expect me to do something on his behalf and not say no.

"You will have to come tomorrow, after I tell my husband all about this and ask his permission" I replied.

After I explained the situation to my husband he scolded, "No, it is impossible. You know that these people are very easy to die and are liable to put you in trouble. I don't want you to do it; I don't want any misunderstanding with the people."

I told him, "At least I could do the minor things such as purge them with castor oil. They do not even know to take care of themselves or even to take a purge."

"That would kill them since they are not used to it," he warned.

The following day, the same woman came back crying. Since my husband warned me about all the impossibilities about helping her, I became puzzled about how to answer her. Then she started crying again repeating the same words, urging me to help her.

Feeling very sorry for her, I had to harden my heart against my husband's will and told her, "Yes, come tomorrow morning after all the children are at school and I will examine you."

She returned the next morning after my husband had gone to school. When I checked her, I found out that she had caught a bad cold and really needed some treatment. I prepared some herbal medicines and gave them to her. I also gave her a good massage, which we call "anoint." Within a short time, she became completely cured and had gotten back her desire to have more children. She later bore three healthy girls, one after another. Before I treated her she had only two children—one son for her late husband and another with the present husband—and couldn't have any more.

She and her husband asked me how much I charged for the work I had done to heal her. I didn't have the heart to charge for my services because of the great kindness of their parents, Tranquilino and Luciana Chen, during our first visit to the village. We would never forget that it was Tranquilino and Luciana who were my husband's refuge during his time of torment with Jose Oh and his wife when he first went to San Antonio in 1907. However, since they insisted on making an offering, I told them to give me a chicken for my services.

Clemente Holah, Luciana's brother, who was there during our first stay in San Antonio also used to treat us very well. Many times he used to carry us to his plantation to harvest whatever crops we wanted for ourselves. Both Tranquilino and Clemente had already died by the time we returned to San Antonio. Only Luciana and her son Manuel Chen, my husband's godson, were still alive.

Very soon after I cured Luciana, Luteria Bol, the wife of my husband's godson Manuel Chen became my second patient. She had become very ill, soon after her first girl was born. Her mother brought her over all the way from Aguacate where they lived. I also gave her some medicines and massages and in a few days she was healed. Both her mother and she were very pleased and happy and word began to spread in San Antonio, Aguacate, and other villages about what I had done.

One afternoon another Maya lady came to me asking for help with a different case altogether. She had not seen her period for nine months but nothing showed signs of pregnancy. The midwife there had told her that she was with child. When I examined her, I found nothing of the sort. I began to treat her by giving her a purge and other herbal medicines, and also some massages. I continued to examine her as she took the herbal medicines I gave her. Soon she became well and even looked healthier and stronger than she was before. A few months after, she became pregnant indeed and she started to show every day.

At the height of her pregnancy, however, her husband who for some reason or another accused her of having a baby that was not his, tied her hands on the beam of the house one day and gave her a severe beating. She was unable to help herself as both her hands were tied. Immediately after, the woman sent for me. I was shocked to see what had happened. She was weeping and trembling. All over her body was bruised. Her skin was scalded from the burns of hot firewood coals. Sadly and angrily I realized how much beating she had taken from her husband. When I examined her entire body I found out that her unborn child felt lifeless. Furthermore, the poor woman was in so much pain that she could not move for about three days. I spent a lot of time treating her and making sure that she and the baby were well.

One day, after I had treated her I met her husband. With all my anger, I scolded him very harshly. "Don't you know that I have the power to report you to the police and have you put in jail? Suppose your wife had died with this child? Don't you see that you would have killed two instead of one? Don't you see how long your wife was suffering in this bad condition that you brought upon her? You should be thankful that I brought her to back to health."

My angry words at him were so strong that I saw a fright in his face but I reminded him, "Don't you ever even think of doing this to her or anyone again."

There were other times when women visited me to report about their husbands beating them. Some of the complaints from the women made me march to their house and scold their husbands harshly. At first some of the men I scolded would either avoid me or would bow or turn their heads in shame whenever they passed me in the village. But after the scolding, some of them usually changed their ways and behaved themselves. In other cases I would beg my husband to go and talk with them, in order to make sure that they do not beat their wives again. Most times, these men were my husband's former students and they would listen to him with deep respect as a father talking to his children. As a result of what I did, many Maya women were saved from being treated harshly by their husbands. This made many of women feel attached to me and confide about whatever they were going through. I also gained respect from the men.

In the case of this woman, when the time came for the delivery, I noticed that the baby was transverse. It was a good thing that I, as the midwife, was clever enough to save the mother. The baby was stillborn but the mother had seven children afterwards, all of whom I delivered.

From that time, everybody came to me with their health problems — men, women and children, young and old, especially after they had heard about the healing I had done. Some days I got very tired after treating people all day, giving them herbal treatments and massages. On other days I walked to the nearby forest to find the different plants that I needed for treatment. Sometimes some of the women came only to talk about their personal problems and ask me for advice. Even after those long days, I sometimes had to wake up at odd hours of the night and walk through dark trails to reach a home and help a mother deliver her newborn.

I never knew anything much about healing before returning to San Antonio, but nothing is impossible to Almighty God, especially when you put your full faith in Him. Many of the medicines I learned to use came through my praying and through dreams I had of my ancestors guiding me and showing me what to do. After all the hardships and illnesses of my family, a new spirit came over me to heal and that was also what guided me. I also learned some of the herbal remedies from elder family members who used and shared these with me. My younger sister Pastora was also a trained midwife in Punta Gorda and she often shared her knowledge with me. Some the herbal remedies I used were sorosi, ganibisi, apasote to treat worms, China root tea for the blood, fever grass, lime, physic nut, rhuda, oregano, billy web bark, cedar bark, soursop leaves, madre de cacao leaves for baths and many others. Some of the herbs are used alone while some are mixed with others.

When I had difficult cases to heal, I prayed deeply about it before I went to see the patient and trusted that the Lord would guide me to do His will. The more persons I healed, the better I became at knowing what was wrong with others and what medicines to give. Over the years in San Antonio and now in Punta Gorda, I have healed hundreds of persons, some of whom were very sick and almost dead. I have also delivered many, many babies in San Antonio and in Punta Gorda. Thanks to the Lord. His mercy endures forever.

I scarcely like to mention all that I have done, but writing this has compelled me to talk about some of them. Nor do I want to seem like I'm bragging about all that I had gone through. I'm only letting you know some of what took place during our family's long stay at San Antonio.

There were those times when there were so many illnesses in the village that there were one, two or three funerals a day. Most of the people came to me for consolation and advice. They asked what to do or how to treat a patient because they knew nothing at all about health matters. My husband got used to this and was no longer against my work as he was in the beginning. For all those years the entire village depended on my husband for their education and for their church services; they depended on me for their health and for delivering their babies. The men came to him for advice and the women came to me for advice.

Knowing what I did about healing made me realize that in the past there were some people who had become ill and died when they could have been saved. Before my work there, most people who got ill with high fever, loose bowels, vomiting, pains, severe headaches and other illnesses did not get any help. I am always thankful that I was able to heal all those that I did. Sometimes the villagers would also come to ask if I would please go to their homes and pray over their son, mother, husband, brother or whosoever was dying and I would immediately go.

Whenever I got puzzled, I called upon God's holy name for divine aid, saying "O Lord, my God our Saviour, if it be possible, have mercy on thy people. Do not deal with us according to our sins; if it be pleasing to Thee, give me all that is needed that I may help thy people who are now suffering with want. Thy will be done."

After praying deeply, I would get that strong feeling that almost everything was possible. Moreover, we never understood that this might have been a reason for our second coming to San Antonio. Our Lord's work is very wonderful and moves in mysterious ways. His work is wonderful and miraculous, that nobody understands, neither ourselves know the reason for our very close relationship with the Mayas.

The more we continued to be strongly liked and respected by the villagers and have strong influence in their lives, the more this caused a few outsiders, especially two of the priests and a policeman, to be very envious. Maybe God sent us back to His people. All those Mayas in San Antonio that were born between 1932 and up to around 1940 before the health clinic was opened, seemed to bring more work, as it was I who delivered all of them. I also delivered many who were born afterwards, even from other villages and Punta Gorda.

Late one evening, a woman visited my home to report that her son, Ursulo Cucul, was very sick. She said she did not know if he was going to recover.

"Is that so?" I answered her. "How long has it been since your son became sick?"

"He was sick for a long time, even before he became married," was her reply. She said that her son had a baby girl a year old.

Not sure that I had heard her correctly I asked again, "Did you say that he was he sick even before he got married?"

"Yes, but not as sick as he is now," she said as if wanting to argue.

I asked, "But why did you let him marry in this condition?"

She answered, "Because I was afraid that he would die without being married."

The older Mayas believed that if a boy died without being married, he would have to carry a heavy post on his back in the other world after death. For them this post was the foundation of the earth. The people had once told me that whenever there is a heavy storm or when the earth shakes, this means that the boys who die without being married are changing the position of the load they are carrying. They believed that is why it was a curse for a boy to die without being married and that's why they had to marry as soon as possible.

My husband and I had to explain to the family that these are only superstitions. I also told the woman that despite all her beliefs, God is pleased with any boy who dies without being married; such are also the angels of heaven or saints.

I asked the woman how old her son was. It seemed to be a puzzling question to her or maybe she was considering whether or not to answer because she was taking a long time to answer, so I repeated, "How old was your son when he got married?"

"He was only sixteen years old when he got married and he has been married for almost three years," she replied looking unsure of herself.

"Could you please come to my home and see my son?" she pleaded. "Whatever it costs, if he gets better I will pay you, and even give you a little pig. He is the only son I have. The man I have is not his father. If he was the father, perhaps he would look after him a long time ago. Now that this man doesn't take care of my son, it caused us not to have anything."

Feeling very sorry for her I replied, "Yes, I will go tomorrow to see what could be done for him."

The next day after Mr. Enriquez and the older children went to school, I carried little Constantine to the home of the sick. After greeting the family with "Dios", they sat me down and explained what was happening to the boy.

As Ursulo laid in the hammock, I examined him carefully and found that he was indeed very ill. He was bloated and looked as pale as a dead man. His whole body was aching. I opened the young man's eyes and mouth, and squeezed his fingertips. His whole body appeared to be white, with no signs of blood. The palpitation of his heart was very fast. It seemed as though he was also suffering from a liver ailment. From my discussion with the family, I learned that he was forced to work too hard when he was younger and he was often straining himself carrying very heavy loads of firewood or crops from the plantation. Now that he was married, he also had his duties to his wife while still working very hard. The village men's practice of bathing in the cold river immediately after their bodies were hot from hours of working in the blazing heat of the sun must have worsened his condition. Over time all these situations caused him to be like this. After examining him, I was puzzled, and remained silent for a moment not exactly knowing what to do.

"Is he going to die?" his mother asked me as she started to cry when she saw me sitting in silence.

"Nobody could be certain of one's death, only God," I replied.

"Please, please try your best," she replied, "I could pay you if it is God's will that he gain back his health."

I told her that as long as she did not blame me if he died, especially that he was already half dead and could not eat, I would try my best.

"You know it yourself," I said, "if he bears up for three more days, we could hope."

I gave Ursulo some of my herbal treatment to drink and after three days he was beginning to show some slight improvement. He was able to take his nourishment. I suggested to his mother the type of diet he should eat. For example I asked her to give him milk and oats instead of corn tortillas and pepper for breakfast. She told me that maybe she can get the milk, but that they did not have any more money to buy the oats. I told her to soak the corn in water, rub it on the metate, strain it with a cloth and boil to make porridge. I told her to half cool it, mix it with milk and give him to drink, but not to give him tortilla and pepper as that would kill him. She was also not to give him any kind of heavy food. Instead chicken broth without pepper would do. She asked if he could bathe in cold water. I answered no and that she should rub him with the bush medicine I gave her, as that is preferable to strengthen him. I also asked her to warm the mixture a little. I carried on with this case little by little.

On one of my visits, I noticed all the members of the young man's family crying around him. When I asked what was wrong, his mother said that he was dying. He had become too weak. I hurried and gathered some leaves of different medicinal plants and then asked for an egg. I massaged the patient's temple, stomach and wrists with the herbal mix. I also massaged the rest of his body with another mixture of bush medicines and oil to make him sweat out the fever. I had to give him some herbal tonic in between in order to strengthen him.

While taking care of this sick man, I still had to do all my domestic work. I had to take care of the baby, draw water from the river for washing, cooking and drinking and other domestic work while my elder children and husband all went to school.

Sometimes, when I could not go to the patient's home, his mother would come to my house to beg me to continue working with him. She pleaded that I must not become discouraged for her son was getting a little better than how he was and he was beginning to eat well. I continued to take care of the young man for about six months before I noticed that he had gathered some strength to be able to walk to the riverside without resting along the way as he had been doing a bit earlier.

Little by little, the young man got better until he was able to walk to his plantation without rest. Still I continued to treat him and around the eighth month I gave him a good dose of lime purge, a mixture of herbs and lime juice. He drank all within the space of time I told him but this did not purge him. I sent another pint of the mixture with his wife and he drank all but again, nothing happened. When his mother came back to my home again saying that her son did not go out at all, I mixed a stronger and larger dose and gave her, asking that her son drink all. I told her to come back to tell me the result.

She returned to say that the medicine was working because his appetite increased and wanted to know what she should feed him. I reminded her to give him only chicken soup, without such seasoning as hot pepper, or other foods as tomatoes, yams and tortillas, which will be too hard for his stomach. The soup should be made bland with only a pinch of salt, and about three grains of black pepper, onion, garlic for flavor and two leaves of wild coriander. All of these were to keep off the gas from his stomach. I also reminded her to give her son hot or warm food in order to heat up his blood and make him sweat. I instructed her to give her son the purge after a while and that if he felt like resting, he should be allowed to do so without disturbance. I told her I would visit her son the next day.

The following evening I visited the home to see the young man.

"How do you feel now?" I asked as I examined him.

"Very good, Ma," he replied eagerly.

"Did the medicine cause you to go out regularly?" I asked.

Everybody in the home stood up to add full details as he explained what had happened. He explained that when he went to the toilet the first time, the stench and look of what he passed was so bad that he had to keep far away. His mother, his wife and he himself gave evidence. The boy continued saying that he passed out yellow, black and green stool that smelled very offensive. His wife said not even the hogs went near. His mother said that the shiny green black flies chased him far. While they excitedly reported what had happened, the family surrounded me as I sat in one corner of the house.

The young man continued, "I passed bad, Ma."

"What kind?" I asked him.

"Ma something very funny," he replied.

"Like what?" I asked.

"Like the tripe of the gallo," he said, meaning the guts of a foul.

After all these things, he got stronger and stronger. At the end of eight months, he was perfectly well, except that he needed some tonic to build him up some more.

After the young man became well and strong, I decided to tell his mother how much I would charge for my services. As soon as I told them about this, I immediately saw a change in their behaviour. They buried their faces down scarcely caring to look at me. When I reminded them how the sick one was and how well and strong he had gotten, everybody bowed and stared underneath of their eyes and towards each other, and treated me somewhat cold. I could not understand this sudden change in their behavior.

Finally his mother answered, "Hmm, when will I see him better? I never will until he dies."

I was shocked at her reaction since the young man was already walking without rest all about the place and even to his plantation. He was already eating whatever he gets, he was sweating normally, and his blood had returned to normal. Everyone in the village had mentioned that this was the healthiest and strongest that they had ever seen him. After the young man got back his full health, he did not even look at me, not even to tell me thanks.

Upon seeing all these things, I spoke to his mother concerning our agreement since she was the one who asked me to heal her son. I told her that since the young man had gotten better, I thought that it was time enough to settle down to business. She herself saw that it was not a little work that I had done to get him back to health and better than he was.

"Even in my dreams, I fought so hard for him," I explained.

It was then that I admitted to her a vivid dream that I had during the time that I was working on her son to be healed. "I had never told you before but I am telling you now, about a dream I had."

"One night, I dreamt that I went to your house to give some medicine to your son. When I arrived there, I saw a very old woman. I never cared about her. I proceeded to the hammock where your sick son was lying. As I approached him the old woman asked, 'What are you going to do?' I told her that I came to see the sick. She then replied, 'Do not have anything to do with him.' In this dream, I asked the woman, 'Why, what is your reason for saying don't you touch him.' 'I said, no don't touch him, he will be mine,' the woman repeated. 'I will attend to him,' I insisted to the woman in my dream. Suddenly the woman jumped up and wanted to fight me and hold me back. In the dream I very angrily held her by her neck, slapped her, dragged her to the door, kicked her outside and said, 'Now, you just leave me alone to attend to this boy.' Then I returned to the sick, examined him, found his liver was enlarged and knew exactly what to do to treat it."

Believe me; although this dream may sound like a joke, it felt so real that it made me dedicate myself to healing this young man. I believed that the woman I dreamt was like the shadow of death awaiting the young man. It was not only the medicines that I gave but I also prayed a lot and fought with every effort to save this young man's life. All this I told the young man's mother.

I also thanked her very much for the gifts she had given me during the months of treatment—one quart of beans, one rapadura, a pint of lard, ten cents plantains and five cents eggs. I told her that for all I had done over those months, I was only charging her four dollars but that she does not have to pay that amount in full cash. I asked her to just give me two dollars because I needed to give alms or to pay a dollar for the thanksgiving Mass I was offering for his recovery. The other dollar would be to recover what I had spent over those months. I suggested that she could cover the remaining balance of two dollars with one of the little pigs running around her yard as she had promised. That was all I asked for the service I gave. I also reminded her that I would not leave her son and that I would continue to get him some tonic to make sure that he gets the extra strengthening that he wanted. After my explanation, no one answered. They just stared at each other.

Finally the boy's uncle said, "Unless he works to get the money to pay you himself, we don't have anything to give you—not even pigs."

They buried their heads down without saying one word more. I returned home empty handed, disappointed and discouraged. Not one cent was paid to what we had agreed and without hopes of getting anything. After all I did over these months they refused to give me anything. I could not believe that there were such ungrateful and mean persons who would treat you so coldly after you spend so much time to heal them.

I told my husband all about what happened and he scolded me saying, "I told you before not to bother yourself with them. Here you are, just wasting your time. You better stop it. You have more than enough to do at home than to leave your household duties to go waste your labour for nothing."

I consoled myself thinking of Our Lord when He healed the ten lepers; only one returned to give thanks. At the same time, I was also glad to see the young man get back to good health. Through this, God gave me more strength to know and to understand more, and more courage to continue.

Another patient I healed was Gregoria Cortez who was also very sick with abdominal pain and high fever. It was good to see her very healthy and strong again.

I also cured Andrea Chun who was ailing for a long time. Her first daughter was going to school. She said that she had gone to see the bush doctor who gave her a hot water bath and placed fire coal under her bed to make her sweat because she was pale and could not eat. The bush doctor also gave Andrea some of the bush medicine to drink and told her to rest in bed for one week. He charged her four dollars and fifty cents, and one hog. However when she got up, she felt the same. She changed three or more different bush doctors.

Whenever she passed my house, I would always tell her to take care of herself and to do whatever the healers told her. I would be out in the yard washing when I would see her passing to go to the healer.

One day I asked her, "How are you?"

She answered, "I am just the same, I heard about another one, I am going to try again."

I told her, "Yes, be attentive to whatever they say to you." She went all around and couldn't get better. For my part, I only encouraged her to look after her health.

In the long run, she came to me and asked if I could attend to her because she was tired of being sick and not knowing what to do. She almost cried saying that she had spent a lot of money and could not get better. As days passed, she was getting worse. She could not eat; she always felt tired and sleepy, spat regularly and had stomach pains. She and her family have been trying all they could. They would massage her stomach but no matter what they did, she was tired of hot bush baths, their bush medicines and their pressing her stomach.

"I feel as if I am going to faint," she said.

"What kind of sickness did the healers tell you that you have?" I asked.

"They told me that I have bad sickness," she replied.

"But what kind of bad sickness?" I asked.

"I do not know, some tell me that I already got better."

I asked, "Did your husband know about you coming here?"

"Yes," she replied. "It was he who had sent me since the past few days. It was only because he was too busy during those days that he could not come with me," she said.

She said she had promised her husband that she would speak with me.

"When would you have the time to begin to take care of me?" she asked. "My husband told me to tell you not to worry about your payment. If I get better, he will pay you."

You see, these people are altogether different than our people or other people. They seem very slow to come out and say what is happening. When they come to you, sometimes you are not sure why they come and perhaps you would be too busy to ask them as soon as they arrive what you could do for them? They would not explain the purpose of their visit until after the end of a long conversation. In order to win your spirit, they bring gifts of whatever they think you want. In this way, you can seldom deny or say no even though at times you would want to, because you are very tired. On the other hand, some of the natives could turn out to be very hard hearted after you show them so much kindness and go out of your way for them.

Sometimes when you ask those hard-hearted ones for any favor, especially in time of need, you would have to mention God's holy name and all the angels and saints, Blessed Mother of God and St. Joseph in a long conversation before they could say yes or no to you. And even with all that pleading with some people you have done so much for, they would still say no. That's how come my husband sometimes became very annoyed at some of them for breaking their promises at the last minute and refusing to help us on our travels to Punta Gorda.

Anyway, I instructed the woman to come early the following morning on an empty stomach, before she ate anything. She came and I examined her. It was to my great surprise to know that all the medicines she had been taking from the native bush doctors never did her any good. I believe that she had an inflammation of the liver, spleen, stomach and womb. Besides she had worms—either pinworm or hook worm—small straight pointed on both sides. After I gave her some herbal medicine and laxative, she passed out worms by the hundreds for nine days. Believe me, I would never write something false. She had been full of worms. After I treated her, the woman then began to have a good appetite. I then turned to heal her liver, stomach and the spleen with the medicine that I mixed.

For a month after, she passed two or three hook worms every day until she got rid of all of them. With the liver medicine she continued to pass two or three at a time as if the last ones were being squeezed out from the liver until she finally passed none. Next, I took care of inflammation of her womb, the gas pains in her stomach and the cold near the lower part of her abdomen. In eight months, she was completely cured. She looked rosy and strong, gained weight and had a good appetite. Some months later she gave birth to a healthy baby boy.

Her husband was very pleased at her return to good health. In fact, he said that she looked better than she had ever been.

One day he asked, "How much should I pay you for all that you have done for my wife?"

When I told him six dollars, he was very thankful and answered, "Muchas gracias senora. Ahora mi mujer ya esta muy bien. Antes yo boto bastante pistos. Dios me va haber usted."

I answered, "Gracias." I also told him, "Quida la bien para que no vuelva agarar otra enfermedad otro vuelta."

He answered, "Si senora gracias", and bid goodbye saying that he would send his wife with the money to pay me.

Andrea the wife came with the money but just as soon as she was about to give me, she asked me if I could reduce the amount I was charging by almost half. I asked her if it was her husband who told her to try to reduce the charges. She said that it was not her husband but she who was making this suggestion. Upon hearing this, I began to feel the same kind of disappointment about the kind of behavior by those who could really afford to pay for the services

I offered. Many of the poor people who I have healed seem to be the ones who try to offer something from the very little they have but those few who have the means seemed to be very stingy and want to offer the least. Much of what I collect is to use to pay others to gather some of the herbs I needed.

Because Andrea's offer for payment did not come from a grateful heart I told her to keep the money. I told her that I was rather satisfied to get nothing and continue to be a good friend. During all those months that I had been treating her, I had not been given even a cent. She did not seem to realize all that I had to go through to find and mix the right type of herbal treatment that I was giving her over the months. I had gone through this sacrifice because I had sympathized with her. Moreover, the benefit of her health was hers and her household and not mine. In the end, I did not even tell her husband about this.

About a year after her first son was born, she gave birth to a baby boy three months after her husband had died. She continued to stay in perfectly good health with her daughter and two sons.

There was another woman whose name was Luteria Pop who was also sick in bed and could not eat or work. She was spitting all day and night and was very thin. She sent for me.

When I got to her home I asked what the matter was and she replied, "I am going to die. I have no strength, my heart beats too fast, don't you hear it?"

"No," I told her. "How long have you been with these feelings."

"Long, long time I don't feel well since I was breaking corn last year," she replied with a worried, lost look on her face. "Please, in the name of the Good Lord, see what is the matter with me? I've been trying. They told me I have bad sickness. They put me in hot water, make beloria and did all kinds of things. I haven't gotten better, only now feeling worse."

For this bad sickness the bush doctor had spent the night at her house performing some of his secret healing practices. I learned that as part of his secrets, he would kill a chicken if the sick person were a woman or kill a rooster if the sick were a man. After killing the animal the bush doctor would rub the raw blood on the hands, temple, collarbone and the ankle of the sick and say some cabalistic words to complete the cure.

All this did not work for Luteria so she came to me and I cured her using my herbs and my prayers. These are only a few examples of the many people I healed. Word got around about my work and this made more and more people come to see me. Some also came from other villages.

# Appendix 1
# Some Pupils of Andres P. Enriquez*

## San Antonio, Toledo District 1907-1918

| Names of Some Pupils | | |
|---|---|---|
| Bol, Catarino | Chun, Genaro | Paquiul, Celestino |
| Bol, Remigio | Ho, Juan | Paquiul, Marciano |
| Cho, Luis | Ho, Manuel | Paquiul, Telesforo |
| Chun, Alejandro | Hob, Paulino | Salam, Sisto |
| | | |

## Forest Home Village, Toledo District, 1919

| Names of Some Pupils | | |
|---|---|---|
| Coleman, Peter | Tulcey, Thomas | Williams, Dan |
| Parham, Israel | Williams, Henry | |
| Tulcey, Marion | Williams, Joseph | |

## Progresso Village, Corozal District, 1921 - 1929

| Names of Some Pupils | | |
|---|---|---|
| Casanova, Guillermo | Lino, Concepcion | Olivera, Emilia |
| Chuallo, Vidal | Lino, Eusiquia | Olivera, Modesto |
| Chuallo, Francisco | Lino, Guzman | Osario, Tomas |
| Codd, Juanita | Lino, Indalecio | Pasos, Leocardio |
| Dominguez, Francisca | Magana, Andres | Rodriquez, Romulo |
| Duran, Manuel | Magana, Nicanora | Sandoval, Agustina |
| Garcia, Anselmo | Magana, Tomasa | Santos, Jovita |
| Garcia, Jeronimo | Novelo, Fidencio | Santos, Victor |
| Ke, Arturo | Novelo, Ignacio | |
| Ken, Celestino | Novelo, Serafina | |

*These lists of pupils were reconstructed in 1996 by Peter L. Enriquez, the second son of Andres and Jane Enriquez.

## San Antonio Toledo District, 1932 - 1949

| Names of Some Pupils | | |
|---|---|---|
| Acalha, Ignacia | Cho, Justiniano | Cucul, Clara |
| Acalha, Lina | Cho, Ines | Cucul, Juan |
| Ah, Basilio | Cho, Isabel | Cucul, Lucas |
| Ah, Maurico | Cho, Marciana | Cucul, Modesto |
| Asi, Adolfo | Cho, Pedro | Ogaldez, Ignacio |
| Balona, Felipe | Cho, Perfecto | Paquiul, Brigida |
| Bol, Calistro | Cho, Rafael | Paquiul, Romualdo |
| Bol, Clara | Cho, Ramona | Paquiul, Ubaldo |
| Bol, Clemencia | Cho, Susana | Pop, Ramon |
| Bol, Dionicio | Cho, Vicenta | Pop, Santos |
| Bol, Filberto | Cho, Zacarias | Pop, Serafina |
| Bol, Luis | Chol, Oracia | Salam, Alfonso |
| Bol, Telesforo | Chub, Nasario | Salam, Cristobal |
| Bol, Ponciano | Chun, Aurelia | Salam, Edwardo |
| Bol, Rufina | Chun, Bartolo | Salam, Mariano |
| Bolon, Narcia | Chun, Catalina | Salam, Jose |
| Bul, Aurelio | Chun, Guadalupe | Salam, Nieves |
| Bul, Herculano | Chun, Isabella | Salam, Thomas Sr. |
| Bul, Juan | Chun, Juan | Sho, Apolonio |
| Bul, Magarita | Chun, Lucas | Sho, Benedicta |
| Bul, Narciso | Chun, Luis | Sho, Catalino |
| Bul, Prudencio | Chun, Luisa | Sho, Dolores |
| Bul, Simeon | Chun, Maria | Sho, Evaristo |
| Cal, Eusebio | Chun, Maurico | Sho, Ines |
| Castellanos, Teodora | Chun, Micarla | Sho, Isabel |
| Catellanos, Erasmo | Chun, Nocolasa | Sho, Jovita |
| Chiac, Adriano | Chun, Ramon | Sho, Juliana |
| Chiac, Estevan | Chun, Sinforoso | Sho, Justa |
| Chiac, Erasma | Chun, Ubaldo | Sho, Lino |
| Chiac, Juan | Coc, Hilaria | Sho, Rufino |
| Chiac, Patrucino | Coc, Josefa | Teul, Hermenegildo |
| Cho, Adela | Coc, Marciana | Teul, Martin |
| Cho, Agustin | Coc, Priscila | Teul, Teodora |
| Cho, Antanacio | Coc, Remigio | |
| Cho, Gregoria | Cowo, Juana | |

## San Antonio Cayo District, 1949-1950

| Names of Some Pupils | | |
|---|---|---|
| Balona, Jose | Oh, Juliana | Tzib, Bidolfo |
| Canto, Canuto | Shish, Francisco | Tzib, Clemente |
| Chan, Josefa | Trejo, Niafero | |

Peter Luis Enriquez, fifth child of Andres and Jane Enriquez, is seated on the left with fellow teachers: (*standing, far left*) Theodore (Ted) Palacio, (*seated, right*) Mike Daniels

# Appendix 2
# Family Charts

## Parents, Siblings, and Children of Andres Patricio Enriquez

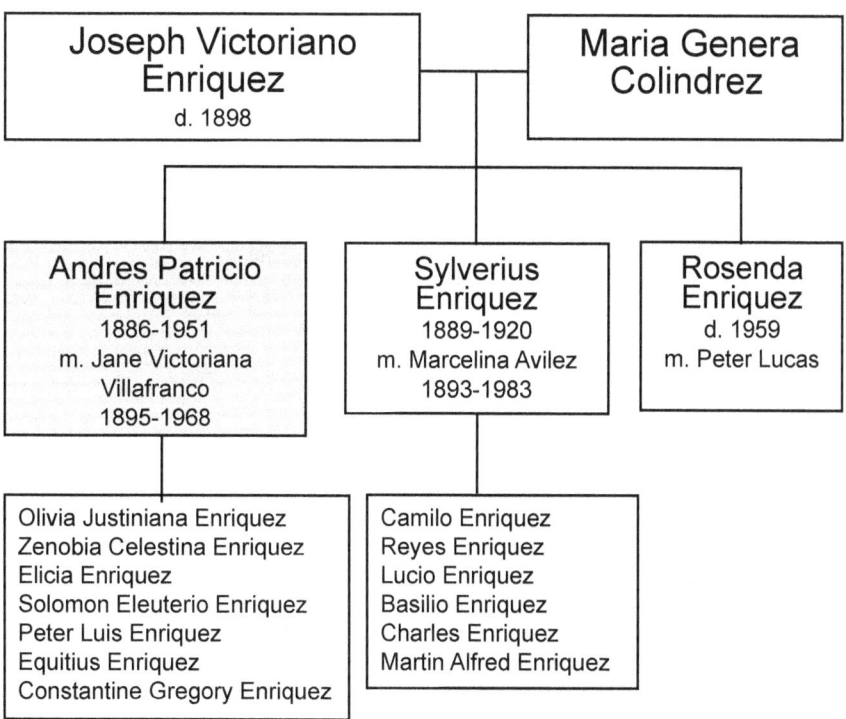

## Parents, Siblings, and Children of Jane Victoriana Villafranco

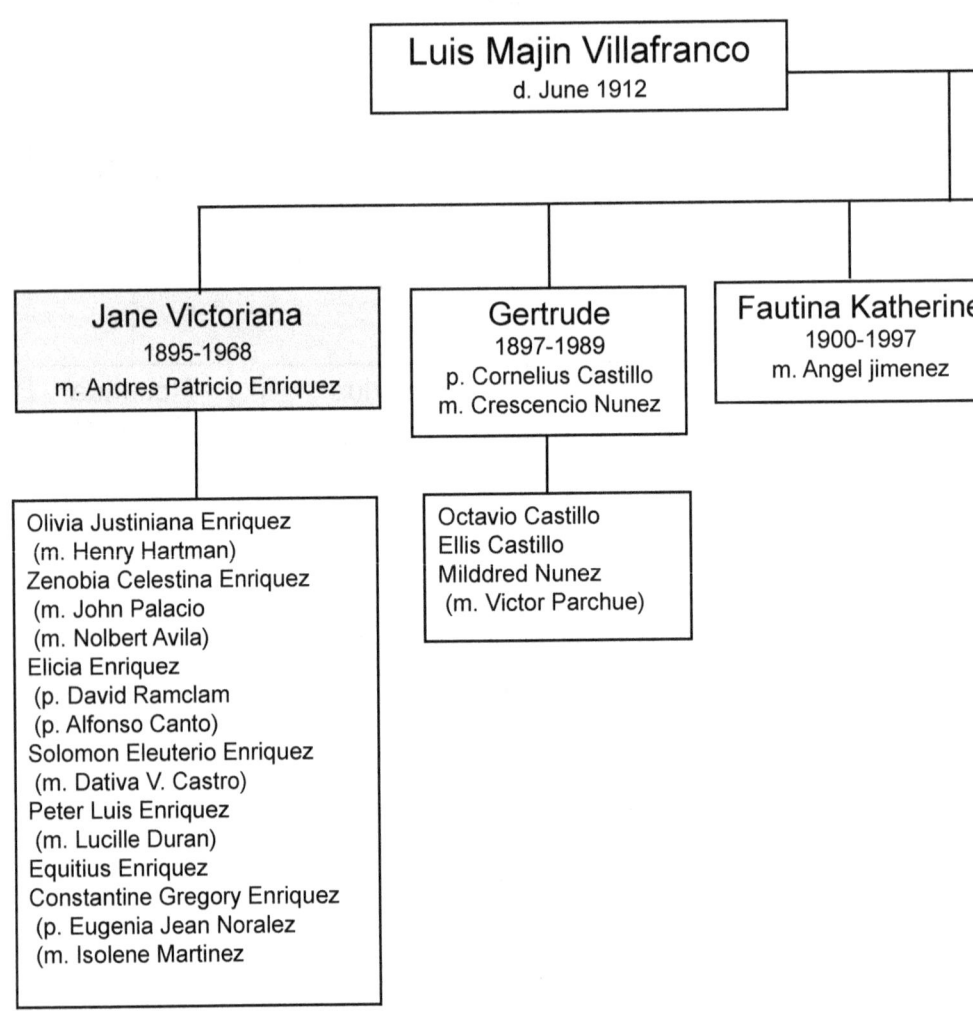

## Appendix 2: Family Charts

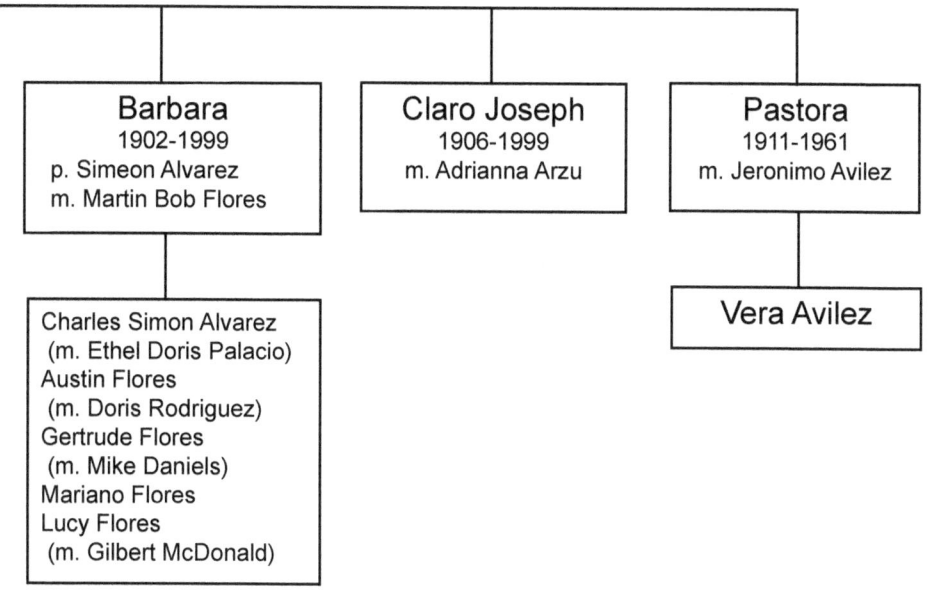

## Children and Grandchildren of Andres and Jane Enriquez

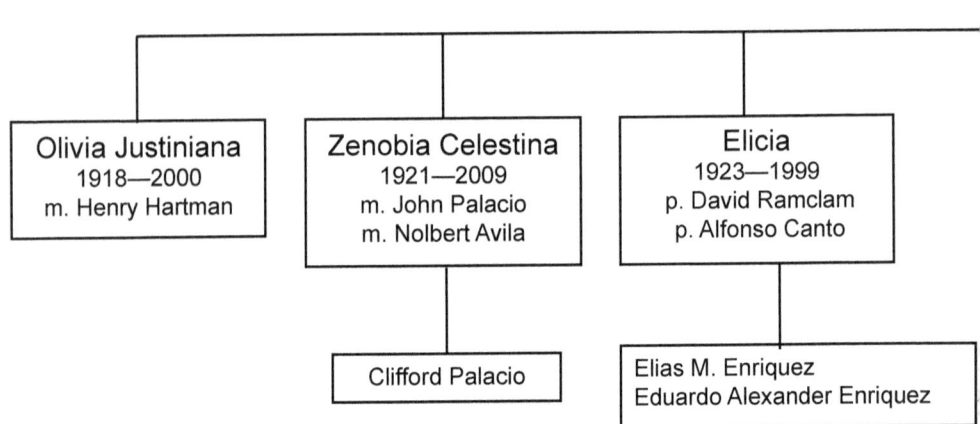

*Appendix 2: Family Charts*

**Jane Victoriana**
1895-1968
m. Andres Patricio Enriquez

**Solomon Eleuterio**
1925—1986
m. Dativa V. Castro

**Peter Luis**
1927—2007
m. Lucille Duran

**Constantine Gregory**
1931—
p. Eugenia Jean Noralez
m. Isolene Martinez

**Equitius**
1929—1931

Jeremy Angelo Enriquez
Violet Jane Enriquez
Cordelia Dolores Enriquez
Juanita Felicia Enriquez
Clara Patricia Enriquez
Ann Marie Enriquez
Solomon Andres Enriquez

Catherine Emily Enriquez
Roy Cuthbert Enriquez
Richard Dennis Enriquez

Jeronimo Lloyd Enriquez
Derrick Enriquez
Kingsley Enriquez
Hubert Enriquez
Eleanor Enriquez
Sarita Enriquez
Constantine Enriquez
Kevin Enriquez

# Appendix 3
# History of the Early Settlement of San Antonio Village
## Andres P. Enriquez

This is an exact reproduction of the history of the people of San Antonio, Toledo, British Honduras, as related to me in the year of Our Lord, one thousand nine hundred and seven to eight, by the following deceased gentlemen: Jose Maria Paquiuil, Benito Tzucanal, Manuel Cho, Leonardo Yacab, Felipe Cho, and Francisco Tesecum. Note that the above-named persons were personal leaders in one form or other in the migration of the above-mentioned people from San Luis, Peten District of Guatemala. If they were leaders in the matter, it stands to reason that their information be considered as first-hand, and more or less reliable and authentic.

"We were simply exasperated by the most cruel and brutal treatment meted out to us at the hands of the officials and subordinates of the Guatemalan government in the village of San Luis in the Peten District of Guatemala, where we then happened to live. During all the years we (as a community) lived there, there was always some group of us that were compelled to some form of service for the government. For example, we had to carry loads of provisions and other burdensome things to distances which took about two months to travel and return to our homes. All that forced labor was unpaid.

This state of affairs was a regular thing throughout all the years. No one could have the time to cultivate and reap his crops due to these circumstances. Very rarely one may be fortunate enough to clear out his plantation spot, but in almost every case it was certain that he wouldn't have the pleasure of seeing that field reaped and stored in barns.

Nothing lasts forever. The people of this community, being tired of this condition, began to grumble first amongst themselves, and then later on, they brought their grievances before the more intelligent members of their group. They, too, saw and felt all that was going on and were complaining among themselves. Things went from bad to worse to such an extent that when nearly all made the same complaint, secret night meetings were held, the objective of which was to decide what was to be done under such brutal oppression. The discussions took place over a period of several months, but in the end, the most intelligent heads (Jose M. Paquiul, RIP being one of them) decided that the party of men should be dispatched secretly to explore the neighbouring country of British Honduras and report on the possibility of establishing a village within its limits where peace and comfort could be enjoyed.

The party of explorers returned to their confederates in San Luis with good news. They reported that there was a spot not very far away, but not (in their opinion) within the Guatemalan territory, which gave good promise of fine agricultural lands, splendid access to water and all the rest of it.

### *The Exodus to British Honduras*

As usual more night meetings were convened to report the findings of the exploration party. After several discussions and exchanging of ideas, it was finally decided that on a certain night, parties of the population should evacuate San Luis with as much of their belongings as possible. They were to travel with certain guides to sojourn to the spot of safety and deliverance. The spot in question was San Antonio Viejo, now called "Pueblo Viejo."

Accordingly as was expected, all parties concerned obeyed the order, and we undertook the journey which took several days. Arriving at San Antonio Viejo, we had no more of the troubles and worries of our last home, and therefore commenced to establish ourselves in the peace and happiness which surrounded us.

We had settled down for some months, when all of a sudden, Guatemalan soldiers and officers began to invade and disturb our peace again. They said that we were still in their territory and as such were still bound to abide by the laws of the state. They went so far as to take and carry away some of our religious statues we had brought with us from San Luis. Fortunately, some of our party managed to go and bring back (by hook or crook) the statues. We were at San Antonio Viejo for about three years when this happened.

These being the case, other more formal meetings were held at San Antonio Viejo to decide on a spot where we should travel to rid ourselves of the disturbance of the Guatemalans. Then parties were sent out again on an exploration expedition, and Aguacate was reported as the next best place.

We then moved as a group to the Aguacate region. At the outset it was discerned that this area, even at its best would not yield us an appreciable living for any prolonged period of time. An attempt was made to conquer the infertility of the soil and its apparent dampness but all was futile. Nobody was satisfied with the results obtained, and, consequently, no time was lost in calling other meetings for the solution of a problem for the final place of establishment of the once wandering people of San Luis.

Another exploration expedition party was appointed which returned with glad news of, "the best that has ever been discovered; rich fertile lands and creeks flowing perpetually." We all packed up our belongings, moved and settled at San Antonio where we are now living.

You will not be so unjust as to blame me for the absence of inaccuracy of dates, for, you must not forget at that time, no record of dates were taken though how the events elapsed were known among the Indians of this tribe. All this must have taken place between the years 1880 to 1884.

Please also note that the above-mentioned deceased gentlemen were my personal friends, and more than that, my protectors, as I was then a mere boy of twenty-one.

A. P. Enriquez, Teacher in Charge
San Antonio Toledo School, British Honduras

It is probable that the school for children was not established until as late as 1890; it is not within my knowledge to report on the number of children then, but what I do know is that around 1905 or so, the school had to be closed down due to lack of interest on the part of the parents who did not care to send their children to school.

In 1907, August, the late Rev. H. G. Huerman, S. J. (deceased) who was then the pastor at Punta Gorda, granted my application to come and reopen the school here. Note that it had been closed for a long time. According, one Rev. Kemphues S.J. (R.I.P) was sent along with me for that purpose; he also made necessary arrangements for my maintenance, etc. etc. From 1907 to 1918 I carried on, except for a break of say, four months. During all this time the school was steadily increasing until at one time before my departure to El Cayo the roll number was one hundred and twenty-five.

In 1906, a new church of metal roofing was built, fire having burned down a former thatch one. No resident priest was sent, but travelling missionaries visited from time to time. It may not be out of place to mention a few of the notable ones, viz, Revs: Fr. A. Averbeck, S. J., C. M. Charroppin, S.J., Louis J. Fusz, S.J., all of whom have passed on to their reward.

The first resident priest to be installed here was the late Rev. Allan A. Stevenson, S. J., who arrived here for that purpose in 1942. He did not last for two years, for sickness and ill-health undermined him until he passed away in 1945 in the U. S.

It was some time after Fr. Stevenson's death that Rev. J. M. Knopp, S.J. was sent to take over the pastorship. He was called away in January 1948. Then followed Frs. Kuinzel, Hodapp and finally here we have today Fr. W. A. Ulrich, S.J. who looks strong enough for his duties.

For a very long time communication with Punta Gorda was made on foot over very rough roads or on horseback. The journey could not be made in a day. It took at least a day and a half.

Today we have the blessing of good enough road for trucks to go over, and all communications are now made on those vehicles, much to the relief of the inhabitants of these remote areas.

Note: This little contribution will, I trust, be of some service to my friends and well-wishers, dray and poor as it is.

Andres P. Enriquez<br>
Nov. 22, 1948<br>
To: Mr. J. W. Forrest, Director of Education<br>
Edn. Office, Belize

P. S. It was my first duty to acknowledge my indebtedness and bow my head in obeisance and gratitude to Mr. Secundino Ogaldez (alive) and Rev. Aloysious Averbeck, S.J. (deceased) who were my teachers, and, consequently, whatever good (if any) I may have done in my career as a teacher reflects on them. The period of time at my disposal for doing this work very limited, and I am asking you, Mr. Forrest, to put this postscript above the last note, since it was due to oversight that it is where you find it.

Thanks.

A.P.E.

> P. S. It was my first duty to acknowledge my indebtedness and bow my head in obeisance and gratitude to Mr Secundino Ogaldez (alive) and the Rev. Aloysious Averbeck, S.J. (deceased) who were my teachers, and, who consequently, whatever good (if any) I may have done in my career as a teacher reflects on them. The period of time at my disposal for doing this work very limited, and I am asking you, Mr Forrest, to put this postscript above the last note, since it was due to an oversight that it is where you find it.
>
> Thanks
>
> A. P. E.

Part of the original manuscript on the *History of San Antonio* written by Andres P. Enriquez.

## Geographical Description of San Antonio by Solomon Enriquez, 1950s

Nestled in a hilly area at the southern part of the Maya Mountains in the Toledo District in British Honduras is the Maya Indian Village of San Antonio with a population of approximately 700. By road it is twenty-one miles from the coastal town of Punta Gorda and is situated at 89° W and 16°15′ North. It is beautifully constructed on hills and valleys and its surroundings afford a fairly picturesque view of ranges of forested natural hills and ancient Maya mounds here and there. In the immediate south of the village is a high slope called *Calvario* after the first erection of a large wooden cross at its summit by the late Father Luis J. Fusz a missionary priest who later became the first resident pastor and who gave it that name.

Dotted on the neighbouring hill slopes are plantations, locally called *milpa*, owned by the natives. A branch of the Moho River, the Murphy Die, runs along the southern side of the village and provides potable water for the natives. A smaller stream flows along the north and north-east side, and empties itself into the Murphy Die. Geologically, the village stands on rather thick layers of strata which make it difficult to build deep foundations for houses. Within the village on the northern side is a small hill range, on the top of which houses are built in the traditional way. Towering on the highest summit at the western side is the police station, the site of which was formerly occupied by the village hall, called *cabildo*.

The village is roughly circular in shape and the houses, which as a rule are thatched cottages, occupy different sites—on hills, on slopes and in valleys. The presence of herbs and fruit trees here and there is the rule rather than the exception. The motor road from Punta Gorda enters the village and terminates on top of the central rising. Public buildings include the Police Station built in 1943, the Nurses Quarters built in 1947, the school and the R.C. mission building built in 1950 and lately in 1952, the Government dispensary.

### *Local Language*

Unlike the Mayas of the northern and western parts of the colony, whose language is of marked difference and heavily intermixed with Spanish, the language of the southern Mayas is relatively pure and more pleasant to the ear. Whether the language has some origination in Latin is a matter of conjecture, but certain words occur in speech, which are equivalent to Latin, such as *et*, an abridged form of *etel*, means "and", *ku* means "what" close to Latin *qui*.

The standard traditional Maya of the south is spoken only in San Antonio and the neighbouring settlements such as Rio Blanco, and Pueblo Viejo. Attempts have been made by the missionary priests aided by Andres P. Enriquez and family, and also some of the natives to write Maya literature but nothing of real substance was completed.

### *Clothing*

As a rule, the women-folk wear a blouse made of white cotton or such other white material, the necks and sleeves of which are embroidered according to individual taste for decoration; and long skirts, fastened to their waists by means of a string, to their toes.

The skirts are generally made of printed material and sometimes silk bright colour worn according to the occasion in which they are used. Girls up to the age of about thirteen years wear ordinary style of clothing sewn locally after which age they change to those of the women. The men and boys wear shirts and trousers generally of local make, also often queer in shape, but of late have been adapting themselves to modern customs of wearing apparel though not yet accustomed to wearing neckties and coats. Boots, shoes, tennis and socks are abundant among the males but very rare among females. The former abundance in use of necklaces among the women and girls is gradually giving way to scarcity but their hair and ears are decorated.

## Editor Jeremy Enriquez

Jeremy A. Enriquez (also known as Jerry A. Enriquez) is the firstborn son of Dativa and Solomon E. Enriquez, the eldest son of Jane and Andres Enriquez, himself a firstborn son. In the lineage of firstborn sons of his family, Jerry Enriquez inherits the distinctive honor of serving as torchbearer of the family's history. His birth and formative years were in Punta Gorda in southern Belize, the town where his family originated. Like his forebears, Jerry A. Enriquez works as an educator, having taught at primary, secondary and tertiary levels of education, nationally and internationally. He also works as a development planning consultant, utilizing his undergraduate and graduate education in the fields of Education, Psychology, Sociology and Development Studies. He has published several articles on national development issues in Belize's leading newspaper, *The Amandala*.

www.ingramcontent.com/pod-product-compliance
Lightning Source LLC
Chambersburg PA
CBHW071202160426
43196CB00011B/2172